The 7 Healing Chakras Workbook

KU-377-301

The 7 Healing Chakras Workbook

Exercises and Meditations for
Unlocking Your Body's
Energy Centers

Brenda Davies, M.D.

Ulysses Press
Berkeley, California

Copyright © 2004 Brenda Davies. All rights reserved under International and Pan-American Copyright Conventions, including the right to reproduce this book or portions thereof in any form whatsoever, except for use by a reviewer in connection with a review.

Published by: Ulysses Press
P.O. Box 3440
Berkeley, CA 94703
www.ulyssespress.com

ISBN10: 1-56975-367-9
ISBN13: 978-1-56975-367-5

Printed in the United States by Bang Printing

10 9 8 7 6 5 4 3

Editorial and production staff: Lynette Ubois, Leslie Henriques, Steven Zah Schwartz,
   Claire Chun, James Meetze
Design: Sarah Levin
Cover Photograph: "Dahlia"/SuperStock

Distributed by Publishers Group West

The author has made every effort to trace copyright owners. Where she has failed, she offers her apologies and undertakes to make proper acknowledgment where possible in reprints.

This book has been written and published strictly for informational purposes, and in no way should it be used as a substitute for consultation with your medical doctor or health care professional. All facts in this book came from medical files, clinical journals, scientific publications, personal interviews, published trade books, self-published materials by experts, magazine articles, and the personal-practice experiences of the authorities quoted or sources cited. You should not consider educational material herein to be the practice of medicine or to replace consultation with a physician or other medical practitioner. The author and publisher are providing you with information in this work so that you can have the knowledge and can choose, at your own risk, to act on that knowledge. The author and publisher also urge all readers to be aware of their health status and to consult health professionals before beginning any health program, including changes in dietary habits.

Table of Contents

Introduction

The miracle is not to fly in the air or walk on water, but to walk on earth.

Chinese Proverb

Since I wrote *The 7 Healing Chakras*, I have wanted to write this companion workbook, though other books that demanded to be written also took my attention. Now however, the time is obviously right, and I am forever grateful to my publishers, Ulysses Press, for this opportunity to make working with *The 7 Healing Chakras* easier. Over the years, *The 7 Healing Chakras* has helped many thousands of people change their lives for the better, and I feel a sense of honor and privilege to have been a fellow traveler on their journey to wholeness. However, as the old adage says, when we hear, we forget; when we see, we remember, but when we do, we understand. I hope the workbook will encourage greater doing and therefore greater understanding!

The plan is that this book will be a companion to *The 7 Healing Chakras*, and therefore much of the original content is condensed here. Please refer to *The 7 Healing Chakras* for the full text.

It was Rumi, the thirteenth-century mystical poet, who said "God has placed a ladder before our feet: we must climb it, step by step." The chakras can be seen as the rungs on that ladder, and working on them to heal and develop them enhances our lives beyond measure and makes things possible that we may only have dreamed of. Here we are—spiritual beings trying our best to be human during this sojourn on the planet. Our physical body is the visible evidence of our incarnation and allows us to experience and share emotions and relate to others who have also chosen to incarnate at this time. The body interprets the physical world with its complex nervous system and senses, and houses our soul. Every cell contains memory and intelligence. But it is as we approach our soul and integrate its gifts into our lives that we come into our own and become the best that we can be.

Though there are chakras lower than the root, and others higher than the crown, in referring to the major seven chakras, we usually have in mind those that we will be dealing with here—the root, sacral, solar plexus, heart, throat, brow and crown. In understanding, healing and developing these, we can touch almost every aspect of our lives—human and spiritual—and effect remarkable growth and change. Qualities that we aspire to are represented here and are available to us—courage, steadfastness, loyalty, love, trustworthiness, understanding, justice, communication, vision and integrity, to name but a few. But also we can move our lives into a state of ongoing inner security, stability, peace and joy; to have, as our natural state, great stamina and health; to sustain over years remarkable energy that leaves others around us—and often much younger than us—startled in amazement. We can also begin to live our lives simultaneously as the human beings we have chosen to be and the spiritual beings we truly are. The aim is to remain grounded and "normal" ordinary human beings (read again the Chinese proverb above), while accomplishing the extraordinary. Life will still continue to throw us challenges, which are our major stimulus for growth. However, we start to take them in stride and with gratitude, welcoming the teaching they bring. Doing the work on our chakras keeps us moving, and since we are less likely to sit complacently in one spot, the Universe has less need to prod us to move on. Thus life becomes more smooth and pleasurable, but always with light and shade and movement to remind us that we opted for some restrictions when we opted to become human.

I hope you will enjoy the work here—some of it might be play! I have used most of these exercises myself on and off for years, though also presented here are some new ones I have had fun with. The meditations I love. For me, time spent in active meditation (no, that is not necessarily a contradiction in terms) is such joy, and the benefits so immediate, that I spend some time every day allowing myself this pleasure. Much of the thrust of healing is in forgiveness, and this is a subject that may arise frequently and recurrently in our lives. We may find ourselves working on it day after day as more things from the past come up from deep in our subconscious to demand our attention and tug at our emotions. Even when we think all is clear and we feel at peace, some event—a piece of music, a phone call from someone in our past—may disturb us and give us the dubious gift of helping bring up something as yet unhealed, which we need to forgive in order to free ourselves from the past. Once again we return to the healing meditations or exercises to look at the gift in the situation, how it changed our lives, how it brought us to where we are and precipitated enough pain for us to have to embark on healing ourselves. And so the work goes on—we are like one of those huge and amazing buildings where the painters start at one end and go back as soon as they are finished to start at the beginning again. T. S. Eliot put it much more eloquently:

> We shall not cease from exploration.
> And the end of all our exploring
> Will be to arrive where we started
> And know the place for the first time

The work is only completed when it is time for us to go home.

It has been said that if we approach the Divine by even a hand's breadth, the Divine will approach us by a cubit, and that if we take one step in the direction of the Divine, the Divine will run towards us in welcome. Certainly this is always what I have found. So my hope is that you will step out with courage in the full knowledge that the Divine will be there to greet you and accompany you on your way. I hope that this workbook will be an instrument of your healing and that you will step joyfully toward your natural state of blissfully living your humanity and divinity simultaneously. In the words of Chekhov, "We shall find peace. We shall hear the angels. We shall see the sky sparkling with diamonds." Enjoy your journey and I will look forward to meeting you again along the way.

> *Out beyond ideas of rightdoing and wrongdoing there is a field. I'll meet you there.*
>
> —Rumi

Brenda Davies
November 2003

How to Use this Book

❧

Let us not look back in anger, not forward in fear,
but around in awareness.

JAMES THURBER

This book is intended as a companion to *The 7 Healing Chakras* (Ulysses Press, 2001) and will help you take command of yourself, your health, your relationships and your life. Each of the main chapters of this workbook will give you a quick review of one major chakra, including its site, color, development, special connection with any other chakra, glandular and neurological connection, and also the auric body it is associated with. You will then find a brief review of the functions of the chakra and what is likely to happen if for some reason its development was disrupted. There is also a list of oils and gemstones that may be helpful to use as you work. You will find more detailed information in *The 7 Healing Chakras*, so please keep a copy beside you for when you would like to look something up.

A self-assessment questionnaire in each chapter helps you see at a glance what events in your life may have arisen from problems with this particular chakra. The aim is that you will come to know, understand and experience each chakra, healing what has happened in your life thus far and letting go of any guilt or shame. You will see that many of the things you have done, or illnesses you have suffered, were predictable in the light of your earlier loss or pain. Just realizing this and being gentle with yourself will help raise your self-esteem and start the healing process.

Each chapter has a section entitled "Now You," which leads you into the healing as you recall and record the events of the initial time of activation and development of the chakra, including the people who were in your life at that time, logging your feelings about them. Though all of our chakras continue to develop throughout our lifetime, each one comes into focus again 30 years later—for example, the root chakra is in focus again from the age of 30 until about 34 and then again at about 60 to 64 years. So you will have the opportunity to look at what was going on at the times of second focus and, if you are old enough (!), the third focus too. For example, if you are in the age group 30 to 34 or 60 to 64, it's likely that you will once again be looking at issues associated with the root chakra, including self-esteem, self-worth and self-confidence. You may be considering a move of some sort as you try to put down roots where you really belong. If you have been depressed or had an addiction, you may try to leave these behind at this time and start to see yourself as unique and important in the world. Recording whatever you can remember or have been told about those times brings things to the surface so that they are easier to heal.

If you know there were some extremely difficult things for you at a certain time, such as serious abuse, then do find a friend or helpful therapist to be with you or assist you as you do the essential work. Take your time—you may find yourself working on one particular chakra for weeks or even months—and constantly remind yourself that you have already survived. It is true that some of the events you recall may prompt a flood of emotion, but quickly following that will be a flood of healing too. Only when things are buried or denied is it difficult to bring them to the light of love and healing.

The exercises and meditations will help you do your own healing, while the list of oils and gemstones will add to the completeness of your experience. (Please note that some oils are not recommended for use during pregnancy—see the list at the end of this chapter. If you have a history of cancer, please avoid using clear quartz crystal since it enlivens all our cells, including those we do not want.) It might be helpful to record the meditations or have a friend read them to you slowly. Take plenty of time with each meditation—work slowly and allow yourself time to rest and to note down whatever you need to before going back to your day. I have added some affirmations at the end of each chapter and I encourage you to make some of your own. Finally there is space to make notes about anything you wish.

At various places you will be asked to write about how you feel. However, if we have been blocked for some time, naming our feelings may be difficult. Sometimes, therefore, it helps to make a list of feelings, so that if necessary you can look at the list and choose the one that is closest to what you are experiencing. There are at least 50 feelings you could name and I have no doubt that once you get to 50 you may find yourself playing a little game with yourself to see how many more you can add. (See page 3.)

Creating a Safe Place

Ideally you need a safe, comfortable place to work, even if it is just a chair with a little table or a box covered with a cloth where you can place a glass of water, a notebook and perhaps a candle, a crystal and maybe a flower or a plant. If you have some item that feels very special to you, such as a photograph, a shell or a stone, put these beside you too. You may use oils or incense to keep your atmosphere balanced while hopefully not upsetting anyone else in your environment. If you have access to an aromatherapist, I'm sure she would be happy to mix a blend of oils that are right for you to use for your bath, as a massage oil or to vaporize.

It would be good to have some uninterrupted time, so turning off your cell phone and taking the phone off the hook would be good. If you have children, make sure they are being supervised so that you don't need to worry about them.

FEELINGS LISTS

Why not make your feelings list here? I've put in a few:

1	Daunted!	18		35			
2		19		36			
3		20		37			
4		21		38			
5		22		39			
6	Carefree	23		40			
7		24		41	Furious		
8		25		42			
9		26		43			
10		27		44	Fascinated		
11		28		45			
12		29		46			
13		30	Perplexed	47			
14	Incredulous	31		48			
15		32		49			
16		33	Exasperated	50	Victorious		
17		34					

Affirmations

These are positive statements in the present tense about what we are actively creating in our lives. It is great to create your own, which you might like to use with your workbook or have in your home, office or safe place. Simply dip into them whenever you wish to focus your heart and mind and help you set your intention.

OILS THAT SHOULD NOT BE USED DURING PREGNANCY

(Note that this may not be an all-inclusive list. Please check with your aromatherapist.)

Basil	Calamus	Cedarwood	Clary Sage
Hyssop	Jasmine	Juniper	Marjoram
Melissa	Mugwort	Pennyroyal	Rosemary
Sage	Thyme	Wintergreen	

My dearest hope is that you will enjoy your healing process and come to a place within yourself where you can appreciate all of the richness and joy of a healthy, spiritually adventurous life. Come, let us begin.

CHAPTER ONE

The Root Chakra

∾

You are here in order to enable the world to live more amply, with greater vision, with a spirit of hope and achievement. You are here to enrich the world and you impoverish yourself if you forget the errand.

WOODROW WILSON

The root chakra is the first of the major chakras to be activated and develop, and its health predicts how we feel about ourselves, the world and our place in it. We have the capacity to embrace life in all its kaleidoscopic glory, cherishing ourselves as amazing spiritual beings here in human form. We have the capacity to be secure and self-confident even when things are difficult, knowing we will survive.

What You Can Hope to Gain by Working with Your Root Chakra

- An improvement in your general energy and sense of well-being
- A greater sense of inner security and therefore less anxiety and improved sleep
- Grounding, so that rather than just feeling better, you will *be* better and therefore more able to deal with the ups and downs of life
- Acknowledgment of your innate beauty and unique worth, giving you more self-esteem and self-confidence
- The knowledge that you are a magnificent spiritual being essential to the total universal plan, and that your contribution, whatever it may be, is worthwhile and unique
- Security in your own identity and joy in the success and empowerment of others
- The abolition of guilt and shame about what has happened in your life thus far, and confidence in the prospect of better stability and health
- Healing of addictions and unwanted behavior as well as physical complaints associated with the root chakra

Now, why not look at the following questions and assess for yourself the work you need to do here.

SELF-ASSESSMENT QUESTIONNAIRE

❏ 1. Have you ever felt that you do not belong anywhere or that you are lonely wherever you are?

❏ 2. Have you ever wanted to escape from your life, either temporarily by drinking, drug taking, gambling or any other addictive behavior, or permanently by committing suicide?

❏ 3. Do you have ambivalence about life, regret about being born and sometimes wish you were dead?

❏ 4. Do you feel disappointed in sex, are impotent or fail to have orgasms?

❏ 5. Did you have some trauma, distress or difficulty, physically or emotionally, between conception and the age of three to five (including birth trauma)?

❏ 6. Do you feel insecure and maybe compensate for that feeling for example by hoarding, buying things you do not really need or refusing to spend your money?

❏ 7. Is your energy low or unpredictable, leaving you often feeling weak, tired or sick?

❏ 8. Do you have physical problems in your legs or feet, or suffer from hemorrhoids or chronic constipation?

❏ 9. Have you suffered from depression?

❏ 10. Have you ever indulged in self-destructive behavior—hurting yourself by cutting, burning, overdosing, etc?

❏ 11. Were you abused—emotionally, sexually or physically—or neglected during your very early years?

❏ 12. Were you separated from a parent before the age of four, for example due to illness (either your own or of one of your parents)?

❏ 13. Were you in an incubator for some time after your birth?

❏ 14. Do you have problems with self-esteem, self-confidence or self-worth?

❏ 15. Have you ever been abusive to other people—emotionally, physically or sexually?

If you answer "yes" to most of the above then you may well have some problem with your root chakra, so now let us learn more about it and how you can start to heal it.

❧ BASICS OF THE ROOT CHAKRA ❧

SITE: About 4 inches in diameter, its physical site is at the perineum—that bit of tissue between anus and scrotum or anus and vagina, and in good health it extends down between your legs, swirling down into the earth in a cone of light.

COLOR: Red—it spins with the same frequency as the ruby gem.

ACTIVATION & DEVELOPMENT: The root chakra is activated immediately after the moment of incarnation, at birth. Its maximal rate of development is during the first few months of life, though focus on the root chakra continues until the age of three to five years. Though development of the whole energy system continues throughout life, the root chakra will become our primary focus again between 30 and 34 and again at 60 to 64 and 90 to 94. At these times we will find ourselves focusing on issues associated with security, belonging, where we want to live and with whom, and how we really feel about ourselves. Our lives may change quite dramatically at these times as we are called to reassess our roots.

GLANDULAR ASSOCIATION: The root chakra is associated with the adrenal glands, which spring into action when our survival is threatened and which govern the fight or flight response when we are in danger.

NEUROLOGICAL CONNECTION: The coccygeal plexus, which supplies the anal and genital region.

ASSOCIATED AURIC BODY: It is associated with the first auric layer, the etheric body, which is bluish gray in color and extends to about one inch from the physical body following all its contours both internally and externally.

SURVIVAL: The root chakra aims to keep us alive no matter what until we complete what we came here to do—hence the association with the adrenal glands.

❧ FUNCTIONS OF THE ROOT CHAKRA ❧

BASIC NEEDS AND INSTINCTS: It governs our basic instincts—eating, drinking, sleeping, sex, self-preservation, shelter and procreation—and thus deals with our sense of inner security and stability.

GROUNDING: It gives us a firm foundation, enabling us to withstand the impact of life and have a sense of belonging and identity.

GOOD JUDGMENT: It assures us of the gift of good judgment, a tool necessary to avoid danger, while still allowing us to be adventurous and take risks.

SELF-CONFIDENCE, SELF-ESTEEM AND SELF-WORTH: It supports our self-confidence, self-esteem and self-worth by reminding us that we are magnificent spiritual beings here being human, and prepares us to deliver our unique message to the world and fulfill our mission as a human being.

PHYSICAL ASPECTS: It governs the lower limbs, the hips, the skeleton and the anus, and also the penis in men. (Women's sexual organs are governed by the sacral chakra—the chakra of the emotions—and therefore most women find sex most satisfying in the context of a loving, nurturing relationship. Men, whose sexual equipment is governed by the root, may see sex is a matter of survival. However, sexuality and sensuality for both men and women are governed by the sacral chakra.)

❧ AND IF THINGS GO WRONG ... ❧

Once we know the functions of any chakra it is easy to work out what might befall us later if it is blocked, weak or underdeveloped.

DEPRESSION AND POOR INNER SECURITY: Contentment and robust health, either physically, emotionally or spiritually, often elude us, and poor self-confidence, low self-esteem and self-worth, with feelings of insecurity, lack of belonging and isolation lead us to suffer depression.

AMBIVALENCE ABOUT SURVIVAL: Depression and isolation result in ambivalence about living and we may tend to opt out. We may do this temporarily, by dissociating emotionally and psychologically, absenting ourselves from the present, or by changing our reality by using alcohol, drugs, gambling, sex, food, etc. Sometimes we may want to leave permanently and suicide becomes an option.

ADDICTIONS AND EATING DISORDERS: Temporary escape via drugs, alcohol, sex, relationships, gambling, work, caffeine, sugar, bingeing, starving or taking care of others so we can avoid ourselves, lead us to the risk of addiction and eating disorders.

CYNICISM AND NEGATIVITY: Chronic lack of contentment and joy lead to cynicism and negativity, which further isolate us, increasing our sense of rejection as we spiral down into a state of permanent disappointment with life.

PEOPLE PLEASING: Fear, rejection or criticism make us desperate for approval. We therefore try to please everyone, becoming irritatingly obsequious, humiliating ourselves by lacking the courage to say what we think and feel, and add to our self-loathing.

"BLACK AND WHITE" THINKING: We are unable to integrate the truth that those we love have faults and those we may not like still have good points. Thus we idealize some and demonize others. This way of thinking may affect not only our relationships, but also our opinions and judgments in every area of our lives.

POOR JUDGMENT AND RISK-TAKING BEHAVIOR: Willingness to take risks is a laudable characteristic, but here we flirt with disaster, angrily testing the universe and ourselves to the limit in a kind of death wish.

PHYSICAL SYMPTOMS: Difficulties with the feet, legs and hips, hemorrhoids, anal fissures and musculoskeletal problems hint that all was not well during the time of root chakra development.

Oils and Gemstones for the Root Chakra

Useful oils and incense include lavender, sandalwood, cedarwood and patchouli. Crystals include smoky quartz, garnet, bloodstone and ruby. All of these gemstones are good for your sexual energy and also promote harmony and balance. The bloodstone also has healing properties for the blood and will help keep you centered while you work. Smoky quartz will help you meditate and help rid you of negativity and skepticism. Garnet balances the libido with the emotional and spiritual components of sex and also has effects on the higher chakras (as do the other crystals) enhancing love, compassion and imagination. Ruby is full of power and passion—just like the root chakra itself!

Now You

Let us have a look at the times in your life where the root chakra is in focus.

Gently now … close your eyes and be aware of your breathing. Then record what comes to mind when you focus on the following times in your life. Do not worry about the second or third focus if you have not yet reached them.

What I remember from the time between birth and three to five years old is: (The major events at this time include your birth of course, but also what was happening to your mother during the pregnancy and how she was afterwards; possibly the birth of other siblings; the relationship between your parents; any death, divorce or separation that occurred then, etc.; perhaps starting kindergarten or primary school, problems arising there and of course any abuse of any kind that happened in this period.)

_____

_____

_____

_____

_____

_____

_____

_____

_____

What I have been told about this time is:

_____

_____

_____

_____

_____

_____

_____

The major people in my life then were:

_____   _____

_____   _____

_____   _____

_____   _____

> *Man has no Body distinct from his Soul; for that called Body is a portion of Soul discerned by the five Senses, the chief inlets of soul in this age.*
> WILLIAM BLAKE

My feelings about this time and the people are:

_____

_____

_____

_____

_____

_____

_____

_____

Second Focus

What was happening in my life between ages 30 and 34:

_____

_____

_____

_____

_____

_____

_____

_____

_____

The major people in my life were:

_____   _____

_____   _____

_____   _____

_____   _____

My feelings about this time and the people are:

_____

_____

_____

_____

_____

_____

_____

_____

_____

_____

Third Focus

What was happening in my life between ages 60 and 64:

_____

_____

_____

_____

_____

_____

_____

_____

> *He who kisses*
> *the joy as it flies*
> *Lives in eter-*
> *nity's sunrise.*
> WILLIAM BLAKE

The major people in my life were:

_____   _____

_____   _____

_____   _____

My feelings about this time and the people are:

_____

_____

_____

_____

_____

_____

_____

Areas of inner neglect and abandonment cry out to you. They are urgent for harvest. Then they can come in out of the false exile of neglect and enter into the temple of belonging, the soul.

JOHN
O'DONOHUE,
ANAM CAR

What All This Gave Me

List here the positive effects on your life—for example: I learned to cope; I learned to be independent; I have the ability to take care of myself and other people; it led me into a healing profession. If you cannot see them now, just skip this section and return to it when it all makes more sense. When you do that, please do both of the meditations again as your capability to forgive, heal and come to inner peace will have increased significantly.

_____

_____

_____

_____

_____

Several exercises, meditations and affirmations now follow to help you heal what you have already uncovered.

Exercises

Now let us start to heal. Please remember also that you have survived and nothing from the past can hurt you now, even though the emotions connected with your experiences may still feel rather raw.

Each of the following exercises can be repeated as often as you like and in any order you choose. Even when you progress to higher chakras, it would still be valuable to incorporate these exercises into your spiritual practice. I work on all my chakras every day despite the fact that I have been working on myself for many years.

Exercise One

You will need:

~ This book, a pen and your safe place

~ If you are lighting candles please be very careful and do not leave them unattended.

~ If you are vaporizing oils, be careful with the burner and the hot water.

~ Give yourself at least 45 minutes when you will not be interrupted—that may mean taking the phone off the hook and switching off your cell phone. Let the outside world take care of itself for a while as you focus on the most important thing in your life—yourself.

List five things that you would like to do—perhaps things that you used to enjoy, for example, spending a day at the beach, having an evening just by yourself curled up with a book, having a massage—or something totally new. Try to include some activity that involves contact with the earth—taking a walk in the forest; walking barefoot on the beach; collecting shells, wildflowers, pine cones or pretty leaves. Maybe you could make a collage with these things when you come home or arrange them in your safe place on a little altar.

1. _____

2. _____

3. _____

4. _____

5. _____

Pause, close your eyes and visualize how it would feel to do each of these things. Record what you visualize each event to be like.

1. _____

_____

2. _____

3. _____

_____

4. _____

_____

5. _____

_____

Now, make a realistic date with yourself to do them. Some you may be able to begin right now, others may take some preparation, but there is always a first step that can begin almost immediately. For example, if you decide to take a vacation, the first step may be getting some travel brochures or scheduling time off from work. If you want to have a massage, you could start to look for a good therapist.

There isn't a person alive who is not capable of greatly contribut ing to the well- being of this planet.

SUSAN JEFFERS

1. _____

2. _____

3. _____

4. _____

5. _____

Transfer these dates into your schedule. Appointments with yourself are as important as appointments with anyone else, so try to respect and keep them. If you do have to break a commitment to yourself (I hope there is a very good reason!), reschedule as soon as possible and fulfill your promise to this very important person—yourself.

When you have completed one of your commitments, come back to this page, add the date and write about how it felt. Compare these feelings with those you expected.

1. _____

_____

2. _____

_____

3. _____

_____

4. _____

_____

5. _____

Is there some discrepancy between how you thought you would feel and how you actually did? How do you account for that? (For example, you had forgotten how much fun it could be to have lunch with a group of friends. Or you realize it has been so long since you had fun that you have actually forgotten how to.)

_____

_____

_____

_____

_____

_____

Exercise Two

It is time for a reward for taking the first step on the journey to self-healing. It can be quite small (or very expensive if you wish!), but it does need to be something significant to your spiritual journey, for example a candle, some oil or incense, or a crystal. Setting a time to go shopping alone for an hour or two would be good. Then take time to make a relationship with your purchase—touch it, feel it, enjoy it, develop a light excited feeling about having it. Appreciating its value will help you appreciate your own.

As my special reward, I bought:

_____

Buying it made me feel:

_____

_____

_____

Exercise Three

- ᑐ What you will need is this book, a pen and your safe place.
- ᑐ Initially, give yourself at least 20 uninterrupted minutes; two or three days later you will need another 20–30 minutes.

Go back and read what you wrote about your early root chakra times (birth to about four or five) as though you were reading about someone else. Imagine a child sitting in front of you who lived through what you lived through. Write a letter to this child, comforting him/her.

Dear _____

_____

_____

_____

_____

_____

_____

_____

_____

_____

_____

_____

_____

_____

Two days later ... Come back to the letter and read it as though it were written to a child you do not know.

After reading it, complete the following:

The feelings I have for the child who lived through this are (for example, compassion, love, awe, sadness):

_____

_____

_____

_____

_____

_____

_____

What I would like to do for this child is (for example hug her, take her hand, look after her—thoughts of revenge or retaliation do not belong here and would only result in further harm, on a soul level at least):

_____

_____

_____

_____

_____

_____

_____

_____

> *Give yourself plenty of time: leave all agendas behind you. Let the neglected presence of your soul come to meet and engage you again.*
>
> JOHN O'DONOHUE, ANAM CARA

Now close your eyes and integrate this child within yourself with as much love and compassion as you can. If you can, make a commitment that you will never hurt her/him, never abandon, never neglect.

If you can, give your child self a hug and be gentle with her/him. Take some time before you return to your day.

Exercise Four

〜 You will need only a place where you can stand or lie.

〜 Allow yourself about 10 minutes of uninterrupted time.

GROUNDING

First of all, a few words about grounding. Grounding acts a bit like a lightning rod assuring our connection with earth and preventing us from drifting off into the ether and losing connection with our humanity. It helps us stay powerful and real, rather than become flaky and fickle. It can be done anytime, anywhere and eventually only takes a few moments or even a single breath. It should be part of our daily routine, ideally first thing in the morning, last thing at night, after meditation or any spiritual work, when we are with someone ill or disturbed, when we feel stressed or off-balance, or when we are under attack—physically, emotionally or spiritually. Note any physical changes as you do it. You may feel as though your weight has shifted—perhaps as though you are resting more on your heels or leaning ever so slightly backwards. You may feel more solid and yet energized and clear; the earth may seem to be coming up to meet you with a powerful current of energy coming right down through your center, as though a breeze is blowing through, bringing you fresh power. Being aware of any new perceptions will help you know when you are grounded.

So … Stand if you can, but if, due to some disability, that is not possible, then sitting or lying will do fine. If for some reason you cannot straighten your spine, do not worry, just skip over the first three sentences of the next paragraph. Energy follows thought, so whatever you visualize will be so.

Standing with your feet flat on the floor, bend your knees slightly so that your weight rests in your pelvis. As you do so, your center of gravity shifts and you may feel slightly heavier (do not worry, you are not!). In this position, your central power channel will be vertical and your chakras aligned. Now take a deep breath, closing your eyes if you wish, and imagine that breath coming down through the middle of you. Breathe it out through your root chakra and the soles of your feet where your plantar chakras (the minor chakras in the soles of your feet) are now opening to the earth too. Imagine that from your root chakra a wonderful ruby red light spins down and into the earth, while spirals of light go down into the earth from the soles of your feet. Feel as though you are sitting on a tripod of light, and that the earth is holding you as though you were sitting in a comfortable chair. Now take another deep breath and this time bring in some white light through the top of your head and visualize it coming down through your central power channel, out through your root chakra and into the earth. Feel a wash of clean fresh energy and know that the earth below and the cosmos above are securely holding you. Just feel that for a moment, then straighten your legs but hold the connection with the earth. Now scan your body and take note of where and how it feels different. Then relax—the earth will hold you. Send it gratitude and an inner smile. When you are ready to move, just do so. You will stay grounded, at least for a while. However, until you become adept at holding your grounding, check as often as it comes to mind whether or not you feel grounded. If you are usually "in your head," it might take you a while to hold your connection. And even when we have been working on ourselves for a long time, things can happen that can blow us off course, so it is good practice to simply be more aware.

Meditations

Please do the meditations in the order they are given, to obtain maximum benefit. You can repeat them as often as you wish, and in future you may want to do only the second meditation. That is fine. If you need to, please read the passage on forgiveness on page viii.

Meditation One

⌒ You will need this book, your journal and a pen and to be in your safe place or another peaceful place of your choosing.

⌒ Give yourself at least 45 uninterrupted minutes.

⌒ ⌒ ⌒

If the first five years of your life were particularly traumatic you may want to have a trusted friend or even your therapist with you while you do these meditations, though you have survived and nothing from the past can harm you now.

Be as comfortable as you can with your spine as erect as possible, using whatever support you need, and be grounded. If you are disabled or for some reason unable to meditate sitting upright, it is possible to do so lying down. Similarly, some people favor the classic cross-legged yoga position.

Now ... take a deep breath and hold the air for a moment to extract the goodness from it. Enjoy, then breathe out, slowly letting any impurities flow out with your breath. Take another deep breath and this time, as you breathe out, allow your body to relax: let your shoul-

It is your involvement with the world that makes you feel you truly belong.
SUSAN JEFFERS,
THOUGHTS OF POWER & LOVE

ders fall, let your chair take your weight, let anything negative flow out through your root chakra and through the soles of your feet. Relax. Repeat again, taking your time. Let yourself breathe in the goodness of the air, the energy that you have created in your safe place … , then when you breathe out, let a wave of relaxation pass through you as you let go of anything you no longer need. Relax.

Now, take your focus back and back and back in time. You are going back to the point of your conception; back to the moment when one cell from your mother and one cell from your father joined and your physical being was created; back to the time when you were warm and safe in your mother's womb. Recall again the events that you remember or have been told about the first five years of your life. Breathe and relax. Take your time. And now, I want you to imagine wrapping your life between birth and about five in a parcel of light and love that you are going to heal. You do not have to remember the details unless you want to …

Now wrap your child self cozily and securely in love … holding gently … holding firmly … holding with healing love and light.

And now, with your child self still held gently but securely, wrapped in love and light in your heart, be gentle with yourself. Take your time. If, at any time, you feel you are not ready to proceed, simply stop, breathe slowly, do some grounding and gently bring your focus back to the room. You do not have to do the whole process today. You can return to it when you are ready.

If you are ready to proceed …

Send out a beam of light to the time, the places, the events, the people of those first five years from conception. A beam of bright, white light to flow into, around, over and through the people, the events, the time and particularly yourself. Now, recognize that you no longer need to carry the past with you. You can come into this moment and move into the rest of your life without dragging the pain of the past with you. You no longer need it. Prepare to let it go forever.

Now with a single breath bring in some love through the top of your head and let it come down to your heart. Let the light envelop everything and every person of that time so that they can be released. Breathe. And as you do so, imagine that the whole burden of that time is being washed away. Finally you can let it go. Release it and let it drift away, bathed in light. You have survived. You are free.

And now, if you can, see that the people who may have hurt you then were living out their own pain and their own processes. They behaved as they did because of their own difficulties. Though you are now released from them, if you can, send out a beam of light and forgive them, let them go so that you no longer need to hold onto anything that will stop you from growing and fulfilling your potential. Breathe. Let yourself feel the freedom of no longer carrying the anger, resentment or pain. Breathe.

And now, if you can, allow yourself to see that whatever happened taught you things you needed to know, things you had set yourself to learn in this lifetime. See that the people who were part of your process were essential to your total life journey. And, if you can, from this highest spiritual perspective, send them love, send them gratitude, and set them free of their burden of guilt. Breathe. Expand. Allow yourself peace and freedom from the past.

Feel cleansed and enjoy the healing. Allow that sense of freedom to percolate through your whole being. Now, allow a beam of light to come into the top of your head and gently spread through you as you enjoy your inner peace. Take your time … enjoy.

There is a pleasure in the pathless woods,
There is a rapture in the lonely shore,
There is society where none intrudes
By the deep sea, and music in its roar.
LORD BYRON

Be aware that your child self is secure in your heart where you can visit as often as you wish, and recommit to taking care of him/her. And when you are ready, prepare to come back to the room.

Bring your focus gently up through your body and back to your heart. Become more aware of your physical presence. Feel your fingers and toes. Bring your focus up now, to behind your eyes, and become more and more aware of your surroundings. Put your arms around your physical body and, gently, when you are ready, open your eyes.

Have a drink of water and record whatever you wish in your journal. Then, take a rest before you do the final root chakra meditation.

Meditation Two

- ∽ You will need your safe place.
- ∽ Give yourself about 30 minutes of uninterrupted time.
- ∽ Take the phone off the hook. Try to have your feet on the floor and your back upright, though if you prefer to lie down, do so.

Now … let your eyes close, and for a moment focus on your breathing and get grounded.

Take a deep breath in and hold it just for a few seconds to allow your lungs to extract the goodness from the air before you breathe all the way out. Let any tension or anxiety flow out with your breath. This time, take a deep breath and feel yourself taking in the healing from the universe, then as you breathe all the way out, let your body relax and allow anything negative to simply flow out through the soles of your feet and your root chakra. Relax …

Now take another deep breath and this time, as you breathe out, let out a long sigh and relax further, visualizing any impurities flowing out of your body in your breath.

Now gently take your focus down through the center of your body until it rests in your pelvis. Imagine your pelvis like a bowl, the bottom of which is sitting at your perineum, the site of your root chakra. Here at the bottom of the beautiful pelvic bowl, there is a wonderful red light, like a deep crimson setting sun. Feel the energy and warmth of this light in your pelvis. See if you can perceive any movement, any change in the color as you focus on it. Send loving feelings to this area and feel the whole area respond with warmth. Focus for as long as you wish on this beautiful, rich, red, swirling light. If you perceive any other color, with a breath allow it to change to red. And if you cannot see a color at all, do not worry. Sometimes the visualization takes practice. It will come.

Now, allow this red light to gently spread down both of your legs, filling your thighs and revitalizing your muscles, tendons, nerves—every cell and every atom of every cell being filled with the light. Let it continue to spread down through your legs, pushing ahead of it any tension, stiffness or anything that blocks its flow. Just breathe away any resistance until there is unobstructed flow of this beautiful energy—warming, cleansing, healing and balancing—filling your legs now.

Going down now, let it enter into your feet, every cell, every atom. When you feel as though your whole legs and feet are filled with the light, let it flow out through the soles of your feet, down into the earth where it forms deep roots anchoring you into the wonderful earth energy, holding you secure and solid in the mother earth.

At the same time now send a root down directly from your root chakra. Down, down into the earth so that you are now supported and rooted in three areas, holding you secure and strong. Feel a warm sense of security, of belonging, of knowing you are part of this planet, this universe. Feel the warmth, security and comfort of belonging here in your chosen place.

Just stay for as long as you wish, holding this connection with the earth, feeling secure, feeling held by the earth. Feel your roots deep down within the body of the living earth. Like a strong tree, you are rooted and steady. You belong.

Now, it is time to allow the earth to nurture you. With a breath, reverse the flow and draw up the healing energy of the earth through the roots that you have sunk deep into it. See this as golden energy, healing energy, vital energy, energy of everything good there ever was, now being given freely to you—to heal you, to make you strong, to make you well. Let this energy now move up through your legs, through your thighs and into the power center you are sitting on—the root chakra. See the golden energy of the earth mingle with the crimson energy of this beautiful spinning chakra—the healing energy of the earth mingling with your own energy. Feel yourself heal as the fresh power comes in to bathe you and make you whole. See the petals of the chakra open even further as you welcome the powerful energy of the earth and allow the healing to occur. Feel yourself rooted to the planet and sense your own power as a living part of the universe being fed by the mother earth …

Savor the energy of the planet as it continues to flow in.

Now, gather up that energy, and with a breath, allow it to gently move up through your body, healing as it goes. Gently, up through every organ, filling you with that same sense of wholeness and belonging. All of you now being filled with the energy of the earth and becoming stronger. Feel yourself fully present in this moment, in your body. Enjoy.

Let the energy continue to gently rise until eventually it sprays out through the top of your head and, like a fountain, it falls gently around you, shimmering through your aura and falling back down to the earth. As you breathe, allow the energy to flow, as you sit now in this living fountain of light, energizing and strengthening you from within and energizing your aura as it falls again back to the earth. As you breathe, feel yourself as part of this living fountain. You may find that the light has taken on a different color. As it rises, it may have become golden, or pink, or white. Allow yourself to be showered in it as the flow continues, healing and cleansing you as you remain rooted to the earth.

Stay for as long as you wish. Enjoy the feeling. Stay rooted and grounded. Centered in your physical body but enjoying the movement, the flow, the neverending motion of the energy as it passes through you. Each time you breathe, be aware of your part in the constant motion, the constant cycle of the universe—energy flowing in, up through you and cascading down around you back to the earth, joining you to the earth. Know that you are where you belong in this moment. In this moment, you have all you need and more. In this moment, you are home with the earth where you belong.

Gradually, when you are ready, allow the flow to slow down and stop while still holding the feelings of security and belonging. You will still remain grounded and in intimate contact with the earth, while you now begin to gently withdraw those roots. With a thought and a breath and giving thanks to the earth for its healing energy, gently, slowly draw up your roots, bringing with them the last bit of energy they can carry. Draw it up your legs and into your pelvis, the crimson light localizing again deep in your pelvis where it resides. Leave your root chakra and the chakras in the soles of your feet open to keep you ever-grounded.

You are now fully within your physical body Affirm your intention to remain grounded and whole.

Silently and reverently say these affirmations:

I am a beloved child of the universe and I deserve love, peace and security.

I open myself to receive the abundance of the universe.

I am open to receive and accept love.

I am open to receive and be nurtured by the powerful energy of the earth.

I am a physical being and value my physical presence.

I resolve to take care of my body and accept it as it is today.

I value my body as the physical temple in which I live and I constantly aim to provide
for its needs in terms of food, rest, stimulation and general nurturing.

Gently add any affirmation you wish, to help you visualize and eventually create a new reality.

When you feel ready, give thanks in whatever way you choose. Then, gently start your return to the room. Be aware of your physical body. Move your fingers and toes and gently stretch. When you are ready, and feeling your feet firmly on the ground, open your eyes and be fully present.

Stay where you are for a little while until you feel ready to move. Have some water or make yourself a warm drink and write in your journal anything you wish to record.

When you feel ready to do so, put your phone back on the hook.

Affirmations

I connect with the earth and am nurtured by it.

I am secure and stable and happy with who I am.

I am content to be incarnated here on earth.

Now make your own affirmations:

_____

_____

_____

_____

_____

_____

Notes

_____

_____

_____

_____

_____

_____

_____

_____

_____

_____

_____

_____

_____

_____

_____

_____

_____

_____

_____

_____

_____

_____

_____

_____

_____

CHAPTER TWO

The Sacral Chakra

❧

By bringing about a change in outlook toward things and events, all phenomena can be sources of happiness.

His Holiness the Dalai Lama

The sacral chakra is the center of our emotions; of flexibility and flow; of inner balance; of tenderness and nurturing. From the stable base of the root chakra, we now begin to flow out to relate to the world.

What You Can Hope to Gain by Working with Your Sacral Chakra

- More flexibility and flow in all areas of your life, including your physical body and its fluid systems
- A greater sense of inner balance, increased vitality and creativity
- Contact with your sexuality and sensuality
- Greater balance and enjoyment in all relationships
- Release of old tension in your body and rigidity in your life, and increasing flexibility in both
- Progress out of inertia and into innovative movement

Now, why not look at the following questions and assess for yourself the work you need to do here.

SELF-ASSESSMENT QUESTIONNAIRE

❑ 1. Do you have difficulty with your sexuality or with giving or receiving sexual pleasure?

❑ 2. Do you have difficulty with being gently touched or nurtured?

❑ 3. Are you unable to perceive yourself as a sensual being and enjoy this aspect of yourself?

❑ 4. Do you have difficulty in nurturing others?

❑ 5. Are you unable to feel in harmony and balance within yourself and within relationships?

❑ 6. Is your stamina or vitality low?

❑ 7. Do you channel your sexual desire into fantasy?

❑ 8. Do you have many sexual partnerships so as to avoid true intimacy with one partner?

❑ 9. Do you have difficulty being flexible and fluid physically, emotionally or in your opinion?

❑ 10. Do you have problems with your bladder, kidneys or urinary tract?

❑ 11. Do you have fluid retention?

❑ 12. Do you have gynecological problems?

❑ 13. Are you legs stiff and do you have problems with dancing or moving gracefully?

❑ 14. Do you suffer lower back pain?

❑ 15. Did you suffer some difficulties or trauma during the period when you were between five and eight years old?

If you answer "yes" to most of the above, you probably have problems with your sacral chakra—now let us learn more about it so you can start to heal it.

✆ BASICS OF THE SACRAL CHAKRA ✆

SITE: The sacral chakra is located about three inches below the navel, in the midline at the front of your body and at the level of the lumbar spine at the back.

COLOR: It spins with a bright translucent orange light.

ACTIVATION & DEVELOPMENT: The sacral chakra begins its development characteristically between the ages of 3 and 5 when the focus shifts from the root chakra. It then remains in focus until about the age of 8. We return to it again at about 34 and focus on it until 38 then again between 64 and 68.

SPECIAL CONNECTIONS: The sacral chakra has a special connection with the throat chakra. The creativity that begins at the sacral chakra is picked up by the throat and communicated to the world as our vocation.

ASSOCIATED SENSE: Taste—not only in terms of food, but also in moving out to taste the world and what it has to offer.

GLANDULAR ASSOCIATION: The ovaries in women and the testicles in men, and also the lymphatic system.

NEUROLOGICAL CONNECTION: Sacral plexus, which supplies the buttocks, thighs and lower limbs and also has a small branch supplying the anal sphincter.

ASSOCIATED AURIC BODY: The second auric layer, the emotional body appears as clouds of pastel colored light, extending to about three-and-a-half inches from the physical body.

～ FUNCTIONS OF THE SACRAL CHAKRA ～

FLUIDITY, FLEXIBILITY AND FLOW: In all areas of our lives—physical, emotional, moods, attitudes and opinions—the healthy sacral chakra guarantees flexibility and flow.

DEVELOPING RELATIONSHIPS: Building on the security, self-esteem and self-confidence of the root chakra and our improved relationship with ourselves, we can now start to reach out into the world and relate to others.

TOUCH, NURTURING AND SENSUAL PLEASURE: Touch is governed by the sacral chakra as well as the heart, and here we start to enjoy the nurturing, sensuality and pleasure of touching and being touched; giving and receiving.

TENDERNESS: We start to know the value of tenderness—both in being tender with others and in being willing to receive tenderness. We also begin to touch our tender emotions.

SEXUAL INTIMACY AND DESIRE: Though at the root chakra sex is biological and functional, its focus on procreation, here sexual intimacy becomes an expression of love and desire, communicating, nurturing and giving mutual pleasure. We move from only expecting satisfaction to wanting to give it.

BONDING AND COMMITMENT: Here bonding and commitment begin to hold those who come together in any form of lasting relationship.

INTERNAL MASCULINE/FEMININE BALANCE: Integration and balance of the masculine and feminine aspects of our nature within ourselves is essential if we are to then find balance within relationships and in our world.

PLEASURE-PAIN PRINCIPLE: The sacral chakra provides us with an early warning system to help us keep on target in our lives by easing the path with pleasure when we are on track and nudging us with emotional pain when we stray.

CREATIVITY: Our creativity is stimulated here, though ideas will be formed at the solar plexus, further enhanced at the throat chakra and manifested at the brow.

TASTE: Now we begin to move out to taste life and all it has to offer.

PHYSICAL ASPECTS: All of our fluid systems, including the urinary system, the lymphatics, and to some extent our circulation, are governed by the sacral chakra, as are the female sexual organs and menstruation.

～ AND IF THINGS GO WRONG ... ～

If there has been trauma at the time of its development or injury later involving the site of the sacral chakra, in adulthood you are likely to have some of the following difficulties.

RIGIDITY AND INFLEXIBILITY: This manifests in all areas of our lives—physical, emotional, intellectual and spiritual, and also in relationship with others as we remain stuck in patterns of thinking, behavior and opinion. Work on both the sacral and solar plexus chakras should help the problem.

FAILURE TO NURTURE: This manifests as inability to nurture both ourselves and others, often to the point of self-neglect and the neglect of others, which can of course become abusive, especially in our dealing with children.

LACK OF BALANCE: Imbalance at the sacral chakra pulls us out of balance in almost every area of our lives. Relationships are particularly affected since the lack of balance of our inner masculine and feminine principles makes it very difficult for us to flow harmoniously with the ever-changing inner equilibrium of others.

LACK OF DESIRE: Our inability to feel desire and pleasure (not only sexually) and loss of interest in sexual intimacy may mar our lives. Depending on the nature of the trauma, however, there may be increased sexual appetite, which, if accompanied by damage to the root chakra, may lead to sexual addiction with self-disgust, frustration and lowered self-esteem as the natural outcome.

LACK OF SEXUAL SATISFACTION: Anorgasmia (failure to have an orgasm), distaste for sex or loss of libido in women and erectile dysfunction in men may occur, with an overall reduction in sensual pleasure.

BLOCKED CREATIVITY: Rather than creativity being awakened here, there may be a dearth of ideas and creative expression.

INABILITY TO TASTE: Not only may we be unable to enjoy our food, but also the other pleasures that life has to offer.

FAILURE TO LISTEN TO THE PLEASURE-PAIN PRINCIPLE: We miss or ignore the signals that our lives are off track and fail to make the changes necessary to bring us back to the pleasure waiting for us in our lives.

SEEKING ATTENTION: Rather then asking for attention in a healthy manner, we may instead whine, become passively aggressive, manipulate or act out our desire to get what we want.

PHYSICAL SYMPTOMS: Stasis in the urinary tract can clog up your water-works and result in fluid retention, recurrent cystitis, infections, kidney stones, nephritis and other such problems. Blocked lymph vessels can cause swelling and tender spots on ankles and legs. Poor peripheral circulation may complicate the picture, and menstrual problems abound, including PMS. There may also be loss of physical flexibility, with stiffness of joints and muscles and lack of graceful movement, particularly in the lower back, hips and legs. Lower back pain is a common problem.

Oils and Gemstones for the Sacral Chakra

Rosemary and amber oils are particularly useful for the sacral chakra, while carnelian, golden topaz and tiger's eye are helpful gemstones. Carnelian, sometimes known as sard, can have a marked effect on emotion and mood, dispelling fear, giving us courage, helping us keep calm, reducing irritability and helping us be cheerful and balanced even when things are difficult. Golden topaz helps us balance our emotions and control our temper, strengthening understanding and helping us move on spiritually. It has a marked effect on creativity (particularly good for artists and musicians), helps us grow and understand new concepts, leading us to emotional and spiritual fulfillment. Golden Tiger's eye has the capacity to balance the masculine and feminine energies—yin and yang—within us, and gently supports us in times of stress. (Tiger's eye is also good for the solar plexus chakra since it has a positive effect on the whole digestive system.) If you have difficulties with sexual intimacy because of sexual abuse in the past, then malachite will help you. Why not carry a piece with you all the time?

Now You

You may not remember the original development of your sacral chakra, but if you do, or if you have heard stories about that time, here is the opportunity to bring to light what needs to be healed. It may be, of course, that your memories are of wonderful things, and if so, please record them too.

Breathe. Take a few deep breaths and record what comes to mind when you focus on these times in your life. Do not worry about the later times if you haven't gotten there yet.

What I remember of the time between four and eight is:

_____

_____

_____

_____

_____

_____

_____

_____

_____

> *The bride comes from the heart of dawn, And the bridegroom from the sunset. There is a wedding in the valley. A day too vast for recording.*
>
> KAHLIL GIBRAN

What I have been told about that time is:

_____

_____

_____

_____

_____

_____

_____

_____

Learn, inner man, to look on your inner woman, the one attained from a thousand natures, the merely attained but not yet beloved form.

RAINER MARIA RILKE

Important people of that time include (these may be family members, teachers, friends, people who loved you or people who may have hurt you):

_____   _____

_____   _____

_____   _____

_____   _____

My feelings about this time and the people are:

_____

_____

_____

_____

_____

_____

_____

_____

_____

_____

_____

_____

_____

_____

Second Focus

What was happening in my life between ages 34 and 38:

_____

_____

_____

_____

_____

_____

_____

_____

_____

_____

The major people in my life were:

_____   _____

_____   _____

_____   _____

_____   _____

My feelings about this time and the people are:

_____

_____

_____

_____

_____

_____

_____

_____

_____

_____

Third Focus

What was happening in my life between ages 64 and 68:

_____

_____

_____

_____

_____

_____

_____

_____

_____

The major people in my life were:

_____   _____

_____   _____

_____   _____

_____   _____

My feelings about this time and the people are:

_____

_____

_____

_____

_____

_____

_____

_____

_____

What All This Gave Me

List here the positive effects on your life—for example: I had to change where I lived; I had to move on to a new career; I got into starting to heal myself; I got so sick that I had to get help. If you cannot see them now, just skip this section and return to it when it all makes more sense. When you do that, please do both of the meditations again as your capability to forgive, heal and come to inner peace will have increased significantly.

_____

_____

_____

_____

_____

_____

> *Creativity is more important than knowledge.*
> ALBERT EINSTEIN

Now you have unearthed some of the issues resulting from events in your life at the time of the natural development of your sacral chakra, let us move on to healing it. Nurturing ourselves is essential groundwork for a healthy and fulfilling life, while it also helps us learn how best to nurture others. There follow several exercises, meditations and affirmations to help you do this.

Exercises

These exercises will help you both emotionally and physically to overcome the pain of the past and also flow into a balanced, harmonious future.

Exercise One

You will need:
- ∾ A good supply of warm water
- ∾ Your bathroom prepared as a sacred space
- ∾ Music
- ∾ Warm towels
- ∾ Massage oil or body lotion
- ∾ At least an hour of uninterrupted time

You may like to do this exercise in the evening before you go to bed.

If the sacral chakra is not well, everything from mood to muscles feel tight and rigid, leaving us feeling tense, irritable, defensive and unable to truly relax. How exhausting! Prepare your bathroom as a sacred space with candles, incense or oils to vaporize, and gentle music. Have some warm towels ready. Prepare a warm bath and make it truly nurturing with oil or floating flowers, or stand in a warm shower holding one of your crystals. Remember that your sacral chakra has a special relationship with your throat chakra, and while you start to relax, say or chant an affirmation or a mantra or simply use your voice gently to tone. Just let yourself relax and flow, physically, emotionally and spiritually blending with the water and letting go of anything you do not need. Imagine that anything that has blocked or hurt you is being released into the water and will flow away, allowing you to emerge cleansed and healed. Any of the following affirmations would be useful, but explore by creating your own.

> *I flow with the natural harmony of the universe and allow myself to accept all the good things it has to offer.*
>
> *All is in Divine order and whatever happens will be just what I need.*
>
> *The natural current and flow of the universe carries me to harmony and balance within myself and with the whole of humanity.*
>
> *I open to my sexuality and am able to enjoy the sensual pleasure for which my body was fashioned.*

Gently wash and massage your body with long strokes up your long bones and circular movements over your joints, affirming your beauty, flexibility and health. Then rest again in the water. Stay as long as you wish, but be careful not to fall asleep in the bath. Pamper yourself with some beautiful lotion and wrap yourself in warm towels or a comfortable robe and rest for a while with the lights down low and in candlelight. Be aware of your body and its intimate connection with your emotions. Allow yourself to get lost in the gentle music and, if you wish, sleep a while or retire to bed. (Remember to blow out your candles.)

Exercise Two

❧ You will need this book and a pen

❧ Give yourself about 30 minutes of uninterrupted time

Write a letter to yourself as though it were to your best friend, telling her how much you care for her and what characteristics you love and respect most. Tell her how proud you are of her and say anything else that is positive, complimentary and loving and make a date to spend time with her. Offer her at least one opportunity to do something really special with you and make a firm commitment to her to take her for a treat. Sign the letter,

Your best friend …

(If you do not have enough space here to complete your letter use a sheet of paper that you can stick into your book later.)

Dear

_____

_____

_____

_____

_____

_____

_____

_____

_____

_____

_____

_____

_____

_____

_____

_____

_____

_____

_____

_____

_____

_____

_____

_____

Exercise Three

⌘ You will need this book and a pen

⌘ Give yourself about 20 minutes of uninterrupted time

Though we instinctively know what our needs are, blocking at the sacral chakra makes it difficult to discern exactly what we do need. For instance, I may think I want food, but if I stop to examine this, I am not hungry at all. Obviously, I have the need for something. Perhaps I am really bored, or angry, or in pain. There are more appropriate actions for me to take than eating. Perhaps I need to meditate or go for a walk, or talk through my anger or ask someone to hug me. But because of past conditioning—for instance when I was upset and tearful as a child I may have been given some candy or an ice cream to pacify me—I now miss some essential cognitive steps and simply go directly to the food rather than look at the cause of my discomfort. The important thing to recognize is that if you feel you need something, you do—though it may not be that chocolate bar! To help at such times of crisis, write a list of possible pleasant diversions—for example, going for a walk, having a swim, listening to some beautiful music, calling a friend. Next time you need something, choose something from your list. Unblocking your sacral chakra and taking a little time to get to know yourself will help you.

Nurturing Activities

_____   _____

_____   _____

_____   _____

_____   _____

_____   _____

_____   _____

_____   _____

_____   _____

_____   _____

_____   _____

Exercise Four

This exercise, which is in two parts, helps you look at balance throughout your life.

PART A

You will need:

❧ This book and a pen

❧ Colored pens/pencils

Let us look first at the possibilities for balance in childhood.

Let us imagine just some of the areas of your life—for example your physical self (P), emotional self (E), intellectual self (I), spiritual self (Sp), social self (S) and relationships (R) and let us put them in Diagram (i) which represents the possibilities in childhood. Ideally, as we develop, all of these parts of ourselves develop equally (see Diagram (ii)). Unfortunately, all too often we find ourselves looking more like a version of Diagram (iii). You may wish during this exercise to look at different aspects of yourself—for example, family life, hobbies, work, service, etc. Now why not complete the exercise.

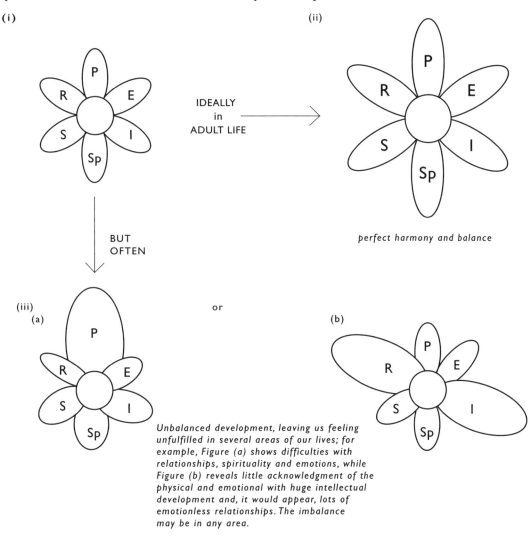

(i)

(ii)

IDEALLY
in
ADULT LIFE

perfect harmony and balance

BUT
OFTEN

(iii)
(a)

or

(b)

Unbalanced development, leaving us feeling unfulfilled in several areas of our lives; for example, Figure (a) shows difficulties with relationships, spirituality and emotions, while Figure (b) reveals little acknowledgment of the physical and emotional with huge intellectual development and, it would appear, lots of emotionless relationships. The imbalance may be in any area.

1. What do you need to do to get your life in balance?
2. Which areas have you neglected?
3. Set goals for areas that need attention and a realistic date for making changes. (Don't expect to do everything at once.)
4. Make a note to come back to this page in six months and draw yourself again.

PART B—INNER MASCULINE/FEMININE BALANCE

Look at the following list of masculine and feminine characteristics and check those you feel you have in abundance. Ideally, we have a balance of characteristics from each column.

POSITIVE MASCULINE PRINCIPLE	POSITIVE FEMININE PRINCIPLE
CHARACTERISTICS INCLUDE:	CHARACTERISTICS INCLUDE:
❏ Action	Creativity ❏
❏ Logic	Art ❏
❏ Organization	Music ❏
❏ Drive	Verbal Skills ❏
❏ Ambition	Nurture ❏
❏ Mathematics and numbers	Spatial awareness ❏
❏ Lists and sequences	Imagination ❏
❏ Linearity	Texture and color ❏
❏ Analysis	Imagery and visualization ❏
❏ Associations	Capacity to see whole picture ❏
❏ Time	Capacity to multitask ❏
❏ Generally associated with action	Generally associated with nurture ❏
❏ Governed by left brain	Governed by right brain ❏

In most healthy men, the masculine principle is to the fore, balanced and supported closely by the feminine principle.

In most healthy women, the reverse is true.

In relationships (whether heterosexual or gay), ideally there is balance within each partner and also in the relationship.

Partner 1   Partner 2

Masculine   [   ]   [   ]   Feminine

Feminine   [   ]   [   ]   Masculine

Here masculine and feminine principles are balanced in each individual and therefore in the relationship. The total is in harmony and balance and each partner can flow within themselves and the relationship.

But if the masculine principle in each partner is overdeveloped, the relationship will look like this:

Partner 1   Partner 2

Masculine   [   ]   [   ]   Masculine

Feminine   [   ]   [   ]   Feminine

There is an excess of masculine characteristics in the above relationship, and it will be tested with aggression, power issues and intellectualization and will lack nurturing for both parties.

	Partner 1	Partner 2	
Feminine			Feminine
Masculine			Masculine

However, if the above is more indicative of the situation the relationship will have little direction, drive and power, but will generally have lots of nurturing from both sides.

If you are in a relationship, or wonder why the last one (or many) failed—draw them here in terms of masculine/feminine balance in yourself and your partner. If you have never had a relationship, please just draw yourself. Refer back to the lists of masculine and feminine qualities to help you be more aware of your inner balance. Use extra paper to work through more relationships if you wish.

ME   PARTNER

What do you need to do within yourself to nurture whichever principle needs help and take command of what may be distorted or overgrown?

For example: Your masculine principle may need to take a self-assertion course in order to be less aggressive.

Your feminine principle may need to learn how to set boundaries.

Your masculine principle may need to learn how to touch and nurture.

Your feminine principle may need to get more organized.

I need to:

_____

_____

_____

_____

_____

_____

(Please note that the only changes you can make are those within yourself. Your partner needs to be in command of his/her own growth. Be encouraged, however, that if you make changes your partner will too, since the energy of your relationship will shift.)

You could read more about this aspect of relationships in my book, *Unlocking the Heart Chakra* (Ulysses Press, 2001).

Meditations

Meditation One

What you will need:
∾ Your sacred space
∾ An hour of uninterrupted time

If you are able to sit erect, please do, but it is important for you to choose a position you will be comfortable in for a considerable period of time.

And now, let us start by focusing on your breathing. As you breathe in, breathe in some beautiful white light through the top of your head, and let it shine down through every cell and every atom of every cell, cleansing, healing and balancing and bringing you into harmony in body, mind and soul. Take another deep breath, and as you do, relax even further, let anything you do not need in this moment simply flow out through your root chakra and the soles of your feet.

In a few moments you are going to begin to heal whatever hurt you between the ages of about four and eight, so just allow yourself to bring those things to mind, though there is no need for them to hurt you now—you have survived and everything is in the past. All that is needed now is for you to heal those things and let them go so that you are not prevented from living your life to the full. Take another deep breath and breathe all the way out.

Gently, gently, gather together the events, the time, the people and the places and breathe some light into them. As you do so, gather them together in a parcel of light that you are going to heal. Take your child self and wrap him/her in love and compassion and hold him/her tenderly and know that she/he is protected.

Now, if you are ready, with a single thought send out healing and forgiveness to that time, to those events and if possible to the people of then. Let light shine around and through all of it so that it can be healed and you can be free. Flow healing light and love to your child self and keep him or her in your heart.

If you are able, but only if you are able, move your forgiveness to a second stage. Move to a spiritual perspective and look at the people and all that happened at that time, seeing that the people did what they did because of their own damage, their own pain and where they were on their path. If you can, see them with compassion and understanding. If you can, forgive them and by doing so set yourself free for once and for all. Let it go. You can be free … Forgive.

Take your time.

And now, if you are able, move to yet a higher stage.

From this spiritual perspective, perhaps you can see that the events that occurred at that time were teaching you things you needed to know in order to become more whole. What you learned is essential to your life's path and perhaps you could see those who were involved in your process as those who were willing to give you the experience you needed. If you can see them as your teachers, perhaps you could now look at them with love and understanding and even gratitude. So if you can, thank them and set them free. Take all the time you need and breathe.

Send gratitude to the highest possible place and become aware again of your child self and note that he/she has a new sense of peace and serenity.

Integrate him/her once more into your whole being and, with a new feeling of tenderness in your heart, make a commitment that you will always cherish your child self, take care of it, love it and never abandon it. Spend as long as you wish until you feel ready to return.

Now, take another deep breath and make sure you are well grounded, and bring your focus to a place behind your closed eyes. Take a deep breath and become fully aware of your physical presence. Feel your fingers, feel your toes and, when you feel fully aware and well-grounded, gently open your eyes.

ᴧ ᴧ ᴧ

Have a drink of water and record whatever you wish in your journal or below.

_____

_____

_____

_____

_____

_____

_____

_____

When we give ourselves the loving we need … our time with others tends to be joyful, graceful, playful, touching—in each moment complete.
AUTHOR UNKNOWN

Meditation Two

Using the same technique, get into a comfortable and relaxed space within yourself. Let go of anything you do not need in this moment and relax.

Now take your focus down through the center of your body, through your heart chakra, your solar plexus and to your sacral chakra. Visualize a beautiful orange light there and allow yourself to wonder at its beauty—shining, swirling light, full of wonderful, radiant energy. Watch it swirling. Feel its movement.

Now allow yourself to gently enter into it … into the orange light. Feel its radiance, its warmth, its energy. Allow yourself to move gently through the light with a sense of delight at being able to explore. Let yourself be carried gently along and you will find that you are moving out through the light and into beautiful clear water. Feel the water gently flowing around you. You are able to breath quite easily. Everything is gently flowing. Feel the water soft on your skin, feel it gently massage your body as it flows around you. Gently, gently flowing. Allow yourself to be carried along. Enjoy the sensation of moving effortlessly in the water.

Move wherever you wish. Feel your body light and flexible. Your body moves like the water, flowing, gently flowing, supple, lithe and gently flowing.

Explore as much as you want to. This beautiful serene place is yours. Feel its peace and its tranquility. Just take your time. And when you are ready, look to your right and you will be delighted to see approaching you through the water a beautiful, powerful yet gentle being. You perceive its power, its magnificence, its vitality and its strong and awesome love for you. Watch it as it moves towards you. Send out a loving, welcoming thought to it. Feel its stimulating energy. This is your masculine principle. Enjoy it. Touch it; welcome it; befriend it. Feel its presence, its benevolence, its beauty and its protection. Feel its amazing power. Enjoy and send a loving message to it. Let it come to rest beside you.

And now, gaze off to your left and you will see approaching you another being. Soft and gentle, beautiful and loving but with strength and wisdom in its vulnerability. You feel its radiance and its gentle but magnificent power. You feel its loving passion, its mysterious beauty. Feel its deep and passionate love for you. Observe it and hold it in your gaze. Send out a warm, loving, welcoming thought to it, for this is your feminine principle. Enjoy its gentleness, its nurture and its serenity. Welcome it. Touch it. Befriend it. Watch its graceful movement and allow it to come to rest beside you as you send out a loving message to it.

And now as you watch, the two move out together, entering into a wonderful, graceful, swirling dance. They move together, flowing around and into each other, swirling, blending, moving apart and then rejoining each other, uniting in wholeness and perfection. Watch them as they move. Feel their love for each other and their love for you. Feel yourself and the whole atmosphere filled with love and joy, feel their vitality, their creativity, their harmony and their balance. And now they are beckoning to you. Come, you are drawn towards them. Mingle and blend with them. You are invited to join with them in their wondrous dance. You unite with them now. Feel your beauty and your own magnificence. Feel your power and your wholeness. Enjoy.

Feel all the flowing fluid within you. Let there be gentle, steady flow within as well as around you. Your circulation is free and easy flowing. Water flows easily in your tissues, cleansing and healing—healing you, healing relationships, healing your life. Deeply cleansing, healing and balancing. Feel the flowing movement of your body, feel your flexibility and the freedom you move with. Feel nurtured. Let yourself receive. Allow yourself the pleasure of being human, being nurtured and being free.

And now, in your wonderful wholeness, with your masculine and your feminine in harmony and balance, with freedom and serenity, let yourself prepare to return. Take your time. Integrating all that you have experienced, move gently back towards the light, the orange light, move gently toward it and then enter it. Flowing, gently flowing through the brilliance, you will find yourself moving back once more out through your sacral chakra. Gently, gently. Relax and savor the moment. Take your time.

Take a nice breath, and when you are ready, gently bring your focus back to your physical presence. Gently back into the room, gently back to this point in time. Bring your focus back to a place behind your closed eyes, and when you are fully aware of your physical presence, take another deep breath. Feel your fingers and your toes and feel your deep connection with the earth. When you are ready, gently, gently open your eyes. Be fully present and grounded. Stay where you are for a moment. Take another deep breath and when you are ready, stretch and move.

Have a drink of water and record whatever you wish in your journal or below.

> *Those who run from pain fall into pain again, and those who escape the snake only meet the dragon.*
> RUMI

Affirmations

My life is in harmony and balance and I flow with nature and with the universe.

My life is a harmonious dance as I share my beauty and nurture with others.

I enjoy my sensuality and sexuality and am free to be who I am.

Make your own affirmations.

_____

_____

_____

_____

_____

_____

> *If I had my life to live over again, I would dare to make more mistakes next time.*
> NADINE SATIR

Notes

_____

_____

_____

_____

_____

_____

_____

_____

_____

_____

_____

_____

CHAPTER THREE

The Solar Plexus Chakra

❧

I dedicate my life to the power within me
Through dedication I unfold naturally to the highest potential of my being.
AUTHOR UNKNOWN

Building on the security of the root chakra and the flexibility of the sacral, we now come to the solar plexus—chakra of power, will, potential, motivation and drive. This is also the chakra of our intellectual selves where we begin to form opinion.

What You Can Hope to Gain by Working with Your Solar Plexus Chakra:

- Well-constructed opinions that are nevertheless flexible
- The ability to harness your will and be dynamic
- Discovery of your inner strength and freedom
- Tenacity to keep going despite difficult life events and circumstances
- Unlimited possibilities—to work, to create change, to become what you want to be, to realize your ambitions, to be happy and to drive your life wherever you want to go
- The transformation of yourself and your life as you move toward peace and contentment

Now, why not look at the following questions and assess for yourself the work you need to do here.

SELF-ASSESSMENT QUESTIONNAIRE

☐ 1. Do you have a fiery, irritable nature?

☐ 2. Do you have difficulty with authority figures, either feeling small and insignificant, or aggressive and rebellious?

☐ 3. Do you feel anger or rage that erupts now and then (maybe after using alcohol) and that you have difficulty in accessing at other times?

☐ 4. Did you suffer distress or trauma between the ages of 8 and 12?

☐ 5. Do you sometimes feel powerless or sometimes so powerful that it almost frightens you?

☐ 6. Have you had difficulty in achieving your potential no matter how hard you work?

☐ 7. Do you have a problem with will, either being weak-willed—often going along with the desires and opinions of others rather than your own—or being willful, going your own way regardless of the consequences?

☐ 8. Do you sometimes feel like a victim at the mercy of other people?

☐ 9. When thwarted or hurt, do you plot ways of getting even?

☐ 10. Do you swing from one extreme to the other—for example, submission to aggression; calm to explosive anger; patience to frustration; love to hate; energy to exhaustion; drive to complacency?

☐ 11. Is it difficult to find prosperity no matter how hard you work or what good things there are in your life?

☐ 12. Do you have difficulty in taking responsibility for your own actions and tend to blame others when things go wrong?

☐ 13. Do you try to control external circumstances, including other people?

☐ 14. Do you have digestive problems, for example ulcers, heartburn or recurrent indigestion or diabetes?

☐ 15. Have you suffered from cancer?

If you answer "yes" to most of the above, then you probably have problems with your solar plexus chakra. Let us learn more about it so you can start to heal it.

〜 BASICS OF THE SOLAR PLEXUS CHAKRA 〜

SITE: In the upper abdomen, between the lower chest and the navel.

COLOR: It spins with yellow light the color of the midday sun.

ACTIVATION & DEVELOPMENT: It is activated and begins its development at 8 and remains in focus until the age of 12. It comes into focus again between 38 and 42 and again between 68 and 72.

SPECIAL CONNECTIONS: The solar plexus chakra has a special connection with the brow chakra since raw gut feelings from the solar plexus are honed there to intuition.

ASSOCIATED SENSE: It is associated with the sense of smell.

GLANDULAR ASSOCIATION: The pancreas, which governs carbohydrate metabolism.

NEUROLOGICAL CONNECTION: The gastric and hypogastric plexi which supply the digestive system.

ASSOCIATED AURIC BODY: This chakra is associated with the mental body, which is yellow in color and extends to about 12–18 inches from the physical body.

〜 FUNCTIONS OF THE SOLAR PLEXUS CHAKRA 〜

POWER, POTENTIAL, PROSPERITY, PASSION, WILL, DRIVE AND AMBITION: It gives us all of these wonderful qualities, and with them, unlimited possibilities—to work, create change, realize who we are and what we want to be, motivated to drive our lives wherever we want to go.

RESPONSIBILITY: Taking responsibility for the fact that we are active players in our lives and have a hand in all that happens to us liberates and empowers us. We are no longer victims of circumstance but are capable of creating a new life strategy, making choices and building a better life.

OPINIONS, LOGIC AND BELIEF: The solar plexus chakra governs our intellectual self, so here we start to develop opinion and logic and formulate our beliefs.

RAW INTUITION: Here we become aware of primitive intuition—hunches or"gut feelings"—which can later be refined at the brow chakra.

PROSPERITY & MANIFESTATION: As we bring together power, potential, will, ambition, drive, purpose and opinion, we sow the seeds of prosperity—abundant energy in all its forms—though its manifestation needs also a healthy brow chakra.

ACCOMMODATING DIFFERENCES: Diversity is a gift that challenges us to grow. The healthy solar plexus chakra helps us become adept at accommodating differences and integrating the new and diverse to enhance and enrich our lives.

PHYSICAL ASPECTS: This chakra governs the health of the digestive tract—stomach, intestines, liver, gall bladder and pancreas.

〜 AND IF THINGS GO WRONG ... 〜

If you suffered trauma between the ages of 8 and 12, it is likely that in adulthood you will suffer some of the following:

MISUSE OF POWER: Perfecting the balance of power between the outside world and ourselves may be a problem, and we may feel disempowered by others or ride roughshod over them, trampling their sensibilities. Our response to authority figures may be to feel small and insignificant or conversely, rebellious, superior and aggressive, neither being appropriate.

HELPLESSNESS: Though we may perceive ourselves as helpless, we never are. We simply use our power maladaptively. Accepting this, we can change our actions and produce a different outcome.

CONTROL: We undermine others by trying to control them and their lives, telling them what to do, how to live and how to behave,

and we become angry or anxious when things do not go exactly as we want them to.

LACK OF AMBITION AND DRIVE: We may lack the motivation, drive and direction to determine our life's course, or conversely we become excessively driven and ambitious.

IRRESPONSIBILITY: We undermine ourselves by seeing ourselves as victims, refusing to take responsibility for our actions and blaming others for our circumstances. Unless we accept responsibility for our lives we take away our power to change them.

"NEGATIVE" EMOTIONS: Anger, rage, bitterness, jealousy, resentment and guilt—the so-called negative emotions—are stored here, often for many years. However, they are highly potent movers if we use them constructively to understand ourselves.

STAGNATION OR OVERFLOW: Stagnation often alternates with overflow—what I call the solar plexus swing—as we flip from

feeling little emotion to an uncontrollable flood; from a lack of motivation to do anything to an occasional burst of energy to the point of exhaustion; from a submissive attitude to an inappropriately aggressive outburst.

STRESS: Stress is common, with irritability, disturbed sleep, lack of enthusiasm, fatigue, exhaustion, poor stamina, weight gain or loss, depression and despair.

PHYSICAL SYMPTOMS: Digestive disorders include indigestion, ulcers, acidity, constipation, diarrhea, irritable bowel syndrome and diverticulosis. Diabetes mellitus may also occur and the liver may be compromised. Gallstones are common. Comfort eating may cause further complications, such as obesity. The association between repressed anger and the development of cancer has been well-documented. (If you have a pattern of alternating constipation and diarrhea, please go to your family doctor and have it checked out.)

Oils and Gemstones for the Solar Plexus Chakra

The most effective oils for the solar plexus are rose and ylang-ylang, and the crystals include amber, topaz, yellow calcite and citrine. Amber prompts the development of a sunny, carefree, optimistic, self-confident attitude, powerful, calm and good humored, with a strong but pliable will. Why do we not all wear it?! Calcite helps develop trust, motivation and positivity, while citrine can produce optimism and openness and may also have such an effect on prosperity that it has been called the abundance stone.

Now You

Now here is your opportunity to bring to light what needs to be healed. Whether your memories are painful or wonderful, please record them here.

Now, take a few deep breaths and record what comes to mind when you focus on these times in your life. Do not worry about the later times if you haven't gotten there yet.

What I remember of the time between eight and twelve is:

_____

_____

_____

_____

_____

_____

_____

_____

What I have been told about that time is:

_____

_____

_____

_____

_____

_____

_____

Anyone can revolt. It is more difficult to silently obey our own inner promptings, and to spend our lives finding sincere and fitting means of expression for our temperament and gifts.
GEORGE RONAULT

Important people of that time include (these may be family members, teachers, friends, people who loved you or people who may have hurt you):

_____   _____

_____   _____

_____   _____

_____   _____

My feelings about this time and the people are:

_____

_____

_____

_____

_____

_____

_____

_____

_____

> *With the realization of one's own potential and self-confidence in one's ability, one can build a better world.*
>
> HIS HOLINESS, THE DALAI LAMA

Second Focus

What was happening in my life between ages 38 and 42:

_____

_____

_____

_____

_____

_____

_____

_____

_____

_____

The major people in my life were:

_____   _____

_____   _____

_____   _____

_____

My feelings about this time and the people are:

_____

_____

_____

_____

_____

_____

_____

_____

_____

> *Man's main task in life is to give birth to himself, to become what he potentially is.*
> ERICH FROMM

Third Focus

What was happening in my life between ages 68 and 72:

_____

_____

_____

_____

_____

_____

_____

_____

_____

The major people in my life are:

_____   _____

_____   _____

_____   _____

_____   _____

My feelings about this time and the people are:

_____

_____

_____

_____

_____

_____

_____

_____

_____

What All This Gave Me

List here the positive effects on your life—for example: I had to change where I lived; I had to move on to a new career; I got into starting to heal myself; I got so sick I had to get help. If you cannot see the positive effects now, just skip this section and return to it when it all makes more sense. When you do that, please do both of the meditations again, as your capacity to forgive, heal and come to inner peace will have increased significantly.

_____

_____

_____

_____

_____

_____

> *Seek not, my soul, the life of the immortals; but enjoy to the full the resources that are within thy reach.*
>
> PINDAR

Now that we have unearthed some of the issues resulting from the events in your life at the time your solar plexus chakra was developing, let us move on to healing it.

Exercises

These exercises will help you overcome the pain of the past both emotionally and physically, and also flow into a balanced, harmonious future.

Exercise One

You will need:

∾ This book and a pen

∾ An hour of uninterrupted time

∾ A writing pad and two envelopes

Nothing can bring you peace but yourself.
EMERSON

You are going to write to each of your parents a letter that you are not going to send. Even if your parents have passed on, this exercise will help heal your relationship with them. In each letter you may say anything you wish—things that you have wanted to say to them but never could; things you have said but went unheard. No one but you ever needs to see the letters, so you do not have to censor what you want to say. You can swear, scream and shout in them if you wish. You can also say you love them and remember the good things. Write until you feel the letter is complete, then leave it where you have good access to it—though preferably somewhere where others do not—and come back and add to it over the next day or so if you want to. When you feel it is really finished, hopefully you can end it by saying that both you and your parents are released from anything either of you did to hurt the other and forgive, but if you are not ready to do that, do not worry. Eventually seal each letter in an envelope.

At the end of your writing session, prepare yourself a lovely bath or shower using some appropriate oil. Once you start to relax, you may suddenly start to release emotion from the past. That is fine. Cry as much as you wish. But if the emotion is anger, please make a commitment not to harm yourself or any property. You may have cried or been angry many times before. This time make it different by bringing in some light and love to heal you when the emotion is over. Love yourself and let it go. Take time before you resume your daily tasks.

You may decide that you never want to open the letters again—and that's okay. But if you do want to, please wait at least a week before you read them again. When you open them you may find that you feel very differently because of the healing that has taken place. Hopefully much of the sting will have dissipated from painful situations. You can then decide to either keep the letters somewhere safe or to ceremoniously destroy them, for example by burning them and releasing all the pain and loss forever.

Exercise Two

You will need:

∾ An extra chair in your safe place

∾ This book and a pen

∾ 45 minutes of uninterrupted time

Go to your safe place and, opposite your seat, arrange another. Close your eyes for a moment and breathe. Then bring to mind your child self of nine or ten years old and imagine him or her sitting on the other chair. Listen quietly, calmly and attentively, with love, compassion, understanding and patience, as your child self tells you how she/he feels about what has been happening to her/him. Asking the child questions if you wish so that you begin to really know her/him and how she/he feels. What does this child need? A hug, praise, encouragement, acknowledgement, love? Judgment, chastisement, violence or punishment are not options here. Take your time. Cry with your child if you need to. When you can, make a commitment that you will love and cherish your child self and never abandon her/him. You need to become your own loving parent now and give her/him what she/he needs. Take your time, and when you are ready, allow your child self to return to your heart where she/he belongs. Welcome your child home.

Do your grounding exercise (see page 15) and be gentle with yourself. Take some time for you and then write your impressions here, recording any relevant conversation between you and your child self and what she/he needs you to do.

_____

_____

_____

_____

_____

_____

_____

_____

> *First keep the peace within yourself, then you can also bring the peace to others.*
> THOMAS A. KEMPS

Now make at least three commitments to yourself. For example:

I commit to being aware of my child self and taking care of him/her.

I commit to working on my solar plexus to ensure my good health.

I commit to reducing the stress in my life.

_____

_____

_____

_____

_____

Exercise Three

You will need:
- ∾ This book and a pen
- ∾ Some index cards
- ∾ 20 minutes of uninterrupted time

Starting with the following affirmations as a guide, adjust them bit by bit until they feel just right for you. Then write them on cards to put in prominent places where you will see them regularly. (My favorite places are always the refrigerator door and my desk drawer. I am certainly going to be there several times most days.)

I take command of my life and respect all others to command their own lives.

I am a powerful being and use my power for my higher good and the higher good of all.

I am open to prosperity in my life. Positive energy in every form flows to me now— love, work, health, stamina, money.

_____

_____

_____

_____

_____

_____

> *Your soul is oftentimes a battlefield, upon which your reason and your judgement wage war against your passion and your appetite … Your reason and your passion are the rudder and the sails of your sea-faring soul.*
>
> KAHLIL GIBRAN

Exercise Four

You will need:
- ∾ This book and a pen
- ∾ Either your safe place or somewhere you will not be disturbed (outside with your feet planted in the earth is good, though you may want to be out of the earshot of others)
- ∾ 30 minutes of uninterrupted time

This exercise will remind you of your power to take command of your life.

Stand with your feet well-planted on the ground and about a shoulder's width apart. Close your eyes and take a few deep breaths, then cup your solar plexus chakra in your hands. Breathe some yellow light into it, and slowly, feeling every word, start to whisper to it. "I am the power."

You may start to feel a physical sensation in your solar plexus as you continue—"I am the power and the peace."

Feel its power begin to grow now, energy building from a trickle to a flood, and feel your body extend to your full height. "I am the power and the peace."

Open your chest and let your shoulders fall. "I am the power and the peace."

Let your chin start to rise as you lift your face to the sky. "I am the power and the peace."

Move your hands away from your solar plexus and reach up to the sky. "I am the power and the peace."

Your voice is stronger and louder now. Shout your message out to the universe if you can. But even if you do not open your throat and use it to the full, you know how your voice would sound and feel if you did. "I am the power and the peace."

Breathe, feeling both your power and your peace. You can face anything. You can overcome anything. You can be all that you need to be. You can learn all that you need to learn. You are responsible for you and no one can ever take that away from you no matter what they do. You are invincible. Your solar plexus is clear and strong. You are in command of yourself and all that happens to you and I hope you will willingly accept that responsibility.

Stay as long as you like and savor every moment of this wonderful powerful yet peaceful time, then when you are ready, make sure you are well-grounded and give thanks. Breathe. Take your time.

Then write your feelings here to remember them, and come back to these even if you feel disempowered.

During this exercise I felt:

_____

_____

_____

_____

_____

_____

Afterwards I felt:

_____

_____

_____

_____

> *I am woman,*
> *hear me roar.*
> HELEN REDDY

Meditations

Meditation One

You will need:

∾ This book and a pen

∾ Your safe place

∾ An hour of uninterrupted time

Spend a little time focusing on your breathing, then use the usual method to achieve a relaxed state.

Then, gently, allow yourself to go back and focus on yourself at the age of about eight. Know that you are fully protected and that anything that might arise is only a memory. Nothing can hurt you now. You have already survived. Let yourself gently scan the time between then and the age of twelve. You have already brought this time to mind; all you need to do now is sweep it all together into a big bundle, which you are then going to cleanse, heal and let go. It is past; you are here.

Now, take your time, and bring in some light through the top of your head and wrap your child self of that time firmly, comfortably and securely and hold her/him in your heart so that she/he knows she/he is safe.

Now send a beam of light to cleanse and heal that time. Let the light shine in through and around it, cleansing and healing it forever … Take your time. If you are able, send forgiveness to the people and the events of that time, releasing yourself from any negative connection with them keeping only the good …

Now, take your time. If you are able, rise to a higher spiritual level and see that the people of that time behaved as they did because of their own pain and process. And if you can, but only if you can, forgive them … (if you cannot, do not worry, go to the end of this part of the meditation).

And now, if you can, raise yourself to see a more complete picture. Maybe you can see that they were a necessary part of your process as you were of theirs. Each of you was simultaneously teaching and learning what you wanted to know in this lifetime. If you can see this, send them gratitude for having played an important part in your life, and finally let them go … (again do not worry if you cannot. You can always come back to this). Breathe.

And now all is clean and clear … Relax and breathe. Now focus on your child self. Wrap him/her in endless love and integrate him/her into your whole being. Feel whole and complete as you integrate this important time into the context of your life thus far.

Take your time, and when you are ready, return to the room … Take a deep breath and fill your physical body with oxygen. Be aware of your physical presence. Move your fingers and toes. Put your arms around your body. Love it … Enjoy your human self. Then, gently return to a place behind your closed eyes, and when you are truly here, make sure you remain grounded, and gently open your eyes and be fully present.

Stretch a little. Have a drink of water. Enter whatever you wish below.

_____

_____

_____

_____

_____

_____

_____

_____

_____

_____

> *A problem is a chance for you to do your best.*
> DUKE ELLINGTON

Meditation Two

You will need:
- ❧ This book and a pen
- ❧ An hour of uninterrupted time

Get comfortable and bring yourself into a relaxed state by focusing on your breathing and letting go of anything negative as you have learned to do.

Allow a wave of beautiful healing light to enter at the top of your head and flow down through you, filling every cell and every atom of every cell, cleansing, healing and balancing you. Every cell is now bathed in light, bringing you into perfect harmony.

And now, take your focus down through the center of your chest and your heart chakra and down again until you focus now on that area in your upper abdomen where your solar plexus lies. Visualize it—a beautiful golden-yellow ball of light, your own personal sun, radiating your brilliance out in all directions, filling you with warmth, filling you with light.

Allow yourself to gaze on its brightness as its radiance enters into all of your cells.

Now as you warm to the light, feel simultaneously its gentleness and its power filling all of you. You are powerful. You are capable and strong. You are able to accomplish whatever you wish to do. Feel the power flowing into all areas of your body. Now let it surge through you—warm waves coursing through you. Feel your renewed motivation to live a healthy and peaceful life, to create an abundance of all kinds of good energy that you can then use for your own good and the good of the world; take responsibility in this moment for all your life from this moment on. Make a pledge that you will continue to use your power wisely.

Enjoy the power and strength that flow through you now. Perceive it with every cell of your body and breathe it out into your aura. Taste it. Enjoy it. Take your time.

Ask that this power may heal old hurt, pain and wounds and also bring you peace and joy for the future. Breathe it now to wherever you wish it to go, radiating like shafts of glowing sunlight. Heal and strengthen every bit of yourself now. Breathe. Take your time.

Stay for as long as you wish in this golden yellow glow. And, when you are ready, knowing that you will forever have this powerhouse deep inside of you and that you can use its limitless power whenever you wish, so long as it is for the higher good of all, start to return. Visualize a beautiful golden-yellow flower over your solar plexus, and with a breath, let its petals close into a tight, tight bud. Hold the power.

And gently now, bring your focus back up though the center of your chest, back up through your throat, back up until once again you are behind your closed eyes. And when you are fully present, feel your physical body and move your fingers and toes. Be well-grounded and fully present, and when you are ready, slowly and gently open your eyes.

Have a stretch and take a drink of water. Record whatever you wish below.

> *Everything that irritates us about others can lead us to an understanding of ourselves.*
>
> CARL JUNG

_____

_____

_____

_____

_____

_____

_____

_____

_____

_____

_____

_____

_____

_____

_____

_____

_____

_____

_____

Affirmations

I am self-assertive in all my dealings with others, whether in conflict or accord. I can say yes or no according to my desire.

I step into my authentic power and enjoy being who I truly am.

I open my heart and mind to receive the power of the Universe, which I use for my higher good and the higher good of all.

I welcome opportunities to fulfill my highest potential.

Make your own affirmations

_____

_____

_____

_____

_____

_____

Notes

_____

_____

_____

_____

_____

_____

_____

_____

_____

_____

_____

> *The most important thing is to be whatever you are without shame.*
> ROD STEIGER

CHAPTER FOUR

The Heart Chakra

Love is a night bent down to be anointed,
A sky turned meadow, and the stars to fireflies.
Love triumphs.
The white and green of love beside a lake,
And the proud majesty of love in tower or balcony;
Love in a garden or in desert untrodden,
Love is our lord and master
We shall pass into the twilight;
Perchance to wake to the dawn of another world.
But love shall stay,
And his finger-marks shall not be erased.

KAHLIL GIBRAN

The heart chakra is the pivotal point of our spiritual ascent, bridging the earthly and the divine as those chakras below it hold us securely in our human state while those above beckon us to the spiritual.

What You Can Hope to Gain by Working with Your Heart Chakra

- Love and compassion for yourself and all the universe
- A lift into universal consciousness
- The capacity to love unconditionally
- The ability to really forgive
- Improvement in all your relationships
- Better cardiac and respiratory health

So let us have a look at how healthy your heart chakra is now before you start the work.

SELF-ASSESSMENT QUESTIONNAIRE

❏ 1. Do you find it difficult to love or feel loved?

❏ 2. Are you negative and pessimistic, or bossy and dictatorial?

❏ 3. Do you get involved in other people's lives and find it difficult to step back and let them make their own mistakes?

❏ 4. Do you feel exhausted, fatigued or drained much of the time?

❏ 5. Are you impatient and intolerant, or so patient and tolerant that people take advantage of you?

❏ 6. Are you difficult to please and often find fault in what people do for you?

❏ 7. Do you find it difficult to let go?

❏ 8. Do your relationships end in acrimony?

❏ 9. Do you quickly "fall in love" and then soon wonder what you ever saw in the person?

❏ 10. Did you suffer distress and trauma between the ages of 12 and 15 or 16?

❏ 11. Do you have difficulty feeling forgiveness, compassion or empathy, or feel so compassionate and empathic that you are dragged down by other people's pain?

❏ 12. Do you have problems with your heart, blood pressure or circulation, or have asthma or respiratory problems?

❏ 13. Are you cut off from the world wondering what love is?

❏ 14. Are you unable to find inner peace?

❏ 15. Have you had any problems with your breasts, including breast cancer?

If you answer "yes" to most of the above, you may have a problem with your heart chakra. When the heart chakra is blocked it often stays stuck open, draining your own energy and leaving you vulnerable to other people's energy and problems. This tendency, suffered by many doctors, nurses, healers, and others in caring professions, leads to burnout. Learning to close your chakras to protect yourself is as important as keeping them free and open.

Protection Method

Whenever you've finished working on yourself, or when you're going to be out in the world, take a few minutes to run through the following:

Take a couple of deep breaths and relax. Imagine a beautiful white flower at the top of your head with its petals wide open. With a thought, see them close. Let the flower become a tight bud. Drop your focus to your brow. See a deep blue flower and let its petals close. Drop your focus to your throat. See a sky-blue flower. Let its petals to close. Drop your focus to your heart, where there is a beautiful green flower. Let its petals close. At your solar plexus there is a yellow flower. Let its petals close to a tight bud. At your sacral chakra there is an orange flower. Let its petals close. Your root chakra stays open to keep you constantly grounded and nourished by the earth. Cross your arms across your chest. Bow your head slightly. Now imagine that there is a beautiful midnight blue cloak beside you. Allow it to drape around you and over your head to fully protect you. Breathe. Know that you are protected.

◡ BASICS OF THE HEART CHAKRA ◡

SITE: In the center of the chest both in front and at the back.

COLOR: Though the classical color of the heart chakra is green, it often appears as pink because of the love that pours through it when it is in good health.

ACTIVATION & DEVELOPMENT: The initial development is between 12 and 16 and it comes into focus again between 42 and 46 and between 72 and 76.

SPECIAL CONNECTIONS: The heart chakra is at the center of the central power channel and is a transitional chakra, connecting our humanity and divinity.

ASSOCIATED SENSE: This chakra is associated with touch, not only in the physical sense, but also in being touched emotionally.

GLANDULAR ASSOCIATION: It is associated with the thymus gland, which is involved with the immune system.

NEUROLOGICAL CONNECTION: The heart chakra has two neurological connections—the pulmonary and cardiac plexi, which are actually extensions of each other and supply the respiratory tract, the heart, the aorta and the pulmonary vein.

ASSOCIATED AURIC BODY: It is associated with the astral body, which appears as clouds of color somewhat similar to the emotional body, but extending to about 30 inches from the physical.

◡ FUNCTIONS OF THE HEART CHAKRA ◡

LOVE: Love at the heart chakra may be personal and focused on the object of love—for example, you love your partner, you love your dog—or universal and without focus—where we are capable of loving everyone, everywhere, including those we know and those we do not. In truly loving relationships we are able to give others space, support and freedom to grow as they (and we) develop and spiritually unfold. We can also divorce the person from their behavior and love them unconditionally even when we dislike what they do, and may have to come to the point of parting.

COMPASSION: We can view others' suffering and distress with understanding and loving concern, while not resorting to sympathy. Sympathy always undermines the other; as we make allowances for them because of their pain, we underestimate who they are and sometimes find ourselves colluding with them, preventing them from learning from the consequences of their actions, and therefore stunting their growth.

EMPATHY: This is the ability to extend ourselves into another person's situation and feel how it must be to experience what they are experiencing, but without getting involved in their process. It is more than simply seeing things from the other's point of view.

ACCEPTANCE: Accepting things as they are right now—including ourselves, other people and their behavior, the weather, world events, etc.—even though we may not like them very much—gives us a piece of solid ground to stand on while we look at what changes we can make. This is not complacency. Having the courage to change ourselves—which is the only thing we have the power to

change—changes everything, since the world constantly reflects us.

PEACE: Only in truly loving and accepting ourselves—body, mind and soul—can we be at peace. Only when we achieve this can we become an instrument of peace and healing in the world. Sadly, many of those who actively petition for peace do so aggressively, and only serve to add their own personal disharmony to the already existing conflict in the world. Only by first healing our own hearts can we help bring peace to the world.

RESPECT: Respect involves having esteem and consideration for others—who they are, what they do, how they feel and how they manage to cope with the challenges in their lives. However, even while respecting someone and honoring them without judgment, I can still decide that I do not want them in my life and separate from them with love and civility.

NON-ATTACHMENT AND FREEDOM: At the heart of real love is freedom and the joy in seeing others grow and fulfill their potential. Love, respect and confidence in the other's process, growth and development holds us together. Attachment simply fosters dependency.

BONDING: When we love someone, we develop bonds between our heart chakras that sustain us and help us remain together even through troubled times. The down side is that when these bonds are torn during separation or at death, we feel the exquisite pain of loss.

GRIEF: As the heart chakra allows us to love deeply, so it allows us the natural function of grief when heart bonds are broken—the classical broken heart. As a rough guide, healthy grief takes about two years to fully heal.

OPTIMISM: Shared with the solar plexus chakra, optimism enables us to see the good in everything and have an attitude of hope. This is neither self-delusion nor seeing the world through rose-colored glasses, for as we love and communicate with the best in people, they reflect our love, and the whole world changes one smile at a time.

FORGIVENESS: The healthy heart allows us to forgive with understanding, love and compassion, recognizing that those who may have hurt us were behaving in a way that simply reflects their own process, experience and emotional state at the time. Forgiveness frees us from the past, releasing energy that may have been tied up for years and allowing us to move on and enjoy the present. For a discussion on the levels of forgiveness you might like to read *Unlocking your Heart Chakra,* (Brenda Davies, Ulysses Press 2001).

THE CAPACITY TO FALL IN LOVE: Often we confuse falling in love with falling into dependence; though they may feel the same initially, the two are very different. Falling in love, where for a while we lose our boundaries and exist almost as one amorphous body of energy, is followed by a shift from drama and chaos into a state of deep loving, with profound contentment and confidence that the love, trust, respect and compassion between us bond us even through times of geographical separation.

PHYSICAL ASSOCIATIONS: The heart chakra governs the health of the physical heart, the major blood vessels, the respiratory system, and also the immune system. The breasts, chest, underarms and palms of the hands are also governed by the heart chakra, as is the thoracic spine.

∽ AND IF THINGS GO WRONG ... ∽

If there were problems between the ages of 12 and 16, there is the likelihood that in adulthood you will have some of the following difficulties.

DIFFICULTIES WITH RELATION-SHIPS: Sustaining mutually supportive loving relationships that respect equality, peace and freedom is tricky, since often recurrent patterns render relationships short-lived and painful or long and drawn-out but never really offering mutual support and nurture.

CODEPENDENCE: Feeling somehow incomplete, we search for people to help us be happy and whole. The resultant codependent relationships, governed by fear, control and entrapment, bring pain and angst to both parties and are doomed to failure usually by the fourth year, if not before, even though they may struggle on for years, as neither partner wants to risk being alone again. The ending of such relationships is often characterized by acrimony, bitterness, violence and threats of, if not actual, revenge. Those who have truly loved do not threaten each other in parting.

NEGATIVITY AND PESSIMISM: Negativity and pessimism replace an optimistic attitude, dragging us down and also affecting our companions who find relaxing and being spontaneous around us increasingly difficult. Disappointment, depression, vulnerability and feelings of rejection ensue as we push people away, depriving ourselves of the closeness we so desperately want and need.

DESTRUCTIVE CRITICISM: Unhappiness with ourselves often leads us to destructively criticize others; of course, in doing so we further isolate ourselves since those we hurt eventually back away.

LACK OF FORGIVENESS AND HOLDING GRUDGES: Since without a healthy heart, forgiveness can never be complete and arguments and disagreements are never really over, grudges may be held for years, energetically holding us in the past and marring our lives.

DEFENSIVENESS AND BEING DIFFICULT TO PLEASE: Insult or slight may be perceived in almost every transaction, and our prickly defensiveness leaves those around us on edge, feeling that no matter what they do, it is never quite right or quite enough. Subtly, but nevertheless aggressively, we put down those we relate to, cutting them to the core with our words, while excusing our cruel behavior by claiming we are very sensitive.

PASSIVE AGGRESSION: This behavior gets 10 out of 10 for damaging others while depriving ourselves of the joy of intimacy. Here, open communication is replaced by ridicule, sarcasm and subtle, snide comments, the real meaning of which is later denied with accusations that the other person must have misunderstood us. Retaliation when challenged often completes the picture. Eventually people in close contact with us become depressed and suffer post traumatic stress disorder, being always on guard and unable to relax while they become confused, doubting their own intuition as their gut tells them one thing and we tell them something else.

DISLIKE, JUDGMENT, HATRED, RETALIATION AND REVENGE: Being unable to perceive the good in all, we often dislike, judge and even hate other people, and in circumstances where we feel hurt, retaliate and possibly exact revenge. The creation of strong and dangerous barriers between us and those we consider to be different and unacceptable becomes the basis of racism and war.

BURNOUT: As we pour out love and energy in an attempt to rescue and heal our partners, our clients and the world in general, we become depleted and exhausted, eventually realizing our worst nightmare in that we are unable to help any more.

RESCUE: Whenever we rescue someone—and by that I mean we do for them something that they could do for themselves, and which would therefore help them grow—we undermine who they are, giving the impression, albeit not spoken, that they are inferior to us and that we can live their lives better than they can. This releases a cascade of behavior which is damaging for both parties, with the results that the rescued person enters a state known as learned helplessness and feels even more inferior, inadequate and dependent, while the other appears superior but sometimes punitive and manipulates with guilt trips when crossed. In fact each is dependent on the other—the one for help and the other for kudos. A good thing to remember is that, no matter how well-meant, the rescue is always an insult! If you would like to read more about this, see *Journey of the Soul* (Brenda Davies, Hodder Mobius, 2002).

PHYSICAL SYMPTOMS: Cardiac and circulatory problems, high blood pressure, angina, arrhythmias and such are all possibilities when the heart chakra is not functioning well. Respiratory problems such as bronchitis, asthma, emphysema, etc., may well occur and since our immune system is compromised infections and autoimmune diseases may follow. Breast problems, including breast cancer, are a function of the disturbed heart chakra.

Oils and Gemstones for the Heart Chakra

Rose, lavender and jasmine oils are useful for this chakra, and the gemstones of choice are rose quartz, aventurine, malachite and jade. Rose quartz helps us love deeply yet gently and with compassion and empathy, while we open to perceive and respond to romance. It also helps us be wise in our choices. Aventurine helps us to be patient, accepting and tolerant while improving our ability to relax and sleep. Malachite deepens compassion and empathy, while also stimulating our wish and ability to learn. Jade regulates heart function, improves vitality and is said to increase longevity.

Now You

Here is the opportunity to bring to light what needs to be healed. So whether your memories are painful and confusing or wonderful and exciting, please record them here.

Okay—let's go …

Breathe. Take a few deep breaths and record what comes to mind when you focus on these times in your life. Do not worry about the later times if you haven't gotten there yet.

What I remember of the time between 12 and 16 is:

_____

_____

_____

_____

_____

_____

_____

_____

When I speak of love in this way, I am not referring to an emotion of sweetness, a feeling of affection, or a sentiment. Often those are simply the responses to an attachment. The love of which I speak is a function, a power, a purity of intent, and the core of honesty of all that is.

GLENDA GREEN

Important people of that time include (these may be family members, teachers, friends, people who loved you or people who may have hurt you):

_____   _____

_____   _____

_____   _____

_____   _____

My feelings about this time and the people are:

_____

_____

_____

_____

_____

_____

_____

_____

_____

_____

Second Focus

What was happening in my life between ages 42 and 46:

_____

_____

_____

_____

_____

_____

_____

_____

_____

> *The man who has no inner life is a slave to his surroundings.*
> HENRI FREDERIC AMIEL

The major people in my life were:

_____   _____

_____   _____

_____   _____

_____   _____

My feelings about this time and the people are:

_____

_____

_____

_____

_____

_____

_____

_____

_____

_____

Third Focus

What was happening in my life between ages 72 and 76:

_____

_____

_____

_____

_____

_____

_____

_____

_____

None but God can satisfy the longings of an immortal soul; that as the heart was made for him, so he only can fill it.
RICHARD CHEVENIX TRENCH

The major people in my life were:

_____   _____

_____   _____

_____   _____

_____   _____

My feelings about this time and the people are:

_____

_____

_____

_____

_____

_____

_____

_____

_____

_____

Compassion is the essence of all authentic spirituality and transcends any definitions and differences of religions.

HIS EMINENCE,
CHAGDUD TULKU
RINPOCHE

What All This Gave Me

List here the *positive* effects on your life—for example: I had to change where I lived; I had to move on to a new career; I got into starting to heal myself; I got so sick that I had to get help. If you cannot see them now, just skip this section and return to it when it all makes more sense. When you do that, please do both of the meditations again, as your capacity to forgive, heal and come to inner peace will have increased significantly.

_____

_____

_____

_____

_____

_____

Now you have had chance to look at your heart chakra and how it performs, let us have a look at how you can start to heal it.

Exercises

These exercises will help you to overcome the pain of the past and flow into a balanced, harmonious future.

Exercise One

You will need:
- ∾ This book, your pen and some extra paper
- ∾ An hour of uninterrupted time

A healthy heart chakra leads to a positive outlook and an optimistic attitude that can change your life. This exercise will help you see the benefits of shifting your attitude and also practical ways to begin to do that.

First let us look at what happens when we are negative.

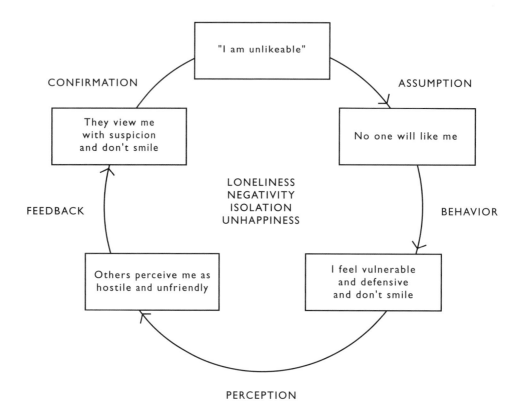

Confrontation with the heart: Standing with courage in front of another speaking our truth from the heart with gentleness, self-assertion and kindness.
BRENDA DAVIES

As you can see from the diagram, a negative thought such as "I am unlikeable" can lead to an assumption that no one likes me. Being prepared for people to dislike and reject me, I feel vulnerable and perhaps hostile or defensive and my behavior reflects this. Naturally this prompts a less-than-friendly response from others and now I have negative feedback, which I interpret as confirmation of my initial belief that I am unlikeable. I am now set up for a whole new cycle of negative thoughts, assumptions, behavior and feedback that I keep on repeating until I eventually find myself lonely and isolated. But actually I set the whole thing up myself without anybody else really doing anything. I set the stage, wrote all the scripts, played all the parts and got to the final curtain by myself!

Let us have a look at some of your thoughts and beliefs about yourself and how they have shaped your life and relationships. You can work through a couple here (for example "I think I am useless") then do some more on your spare paper if you wish. In future, whenever you feel that things are not as you would wish them to be, you can take an honest look at your own attitude, thoughts and beliefs and use this exercise to work through them until you can change your reality.

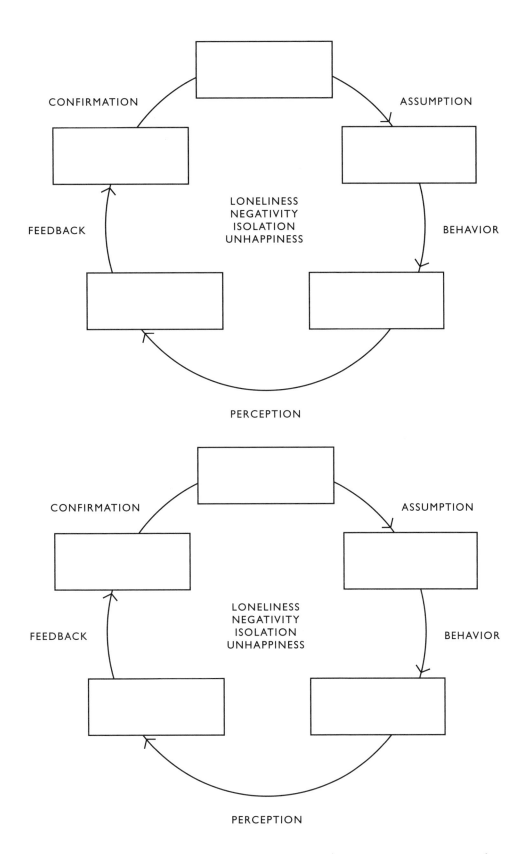

CONFIRMATION

ASSUMPTION

LONELINESS
NEGATIVITY
ISOLATION
UNHAPPINESS

FEEDBACK

BEHAVIOR

PERCEPTION

CONFIRMATION

ASSUMPTION

LONELINESS
NEGATIVITY
ISOLATION
UNHAPPINESS

FEEDBACK

BEHAVIOR

PERCEPTION

Now let us turn the cycle around by opening our heart and taking a risk to have a positive attitude.

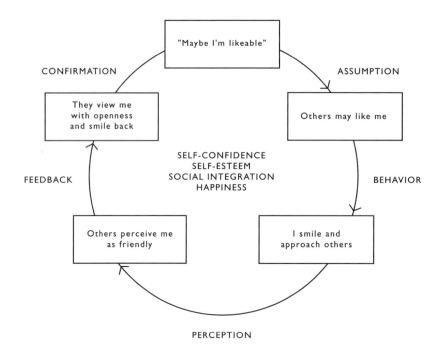

In the first box the thought becomes, "Maybe I am likeable." If so, then my assumption is that others may like me, and so my behavior changes and I smile and surprise, surprise! People smile back. This positive feedback affirms that I am likeable. Now I have a confirmed belief and my self-confidence rises. Now I am willing to take more risks with other people and as my attitude becomes more and more sunny and optimistic, my world expands and my self-esteem continues to grow. I eventually find that my world opens out, leading me to a happier state.

Rework your first examples, having changed the initial thought to a positive one. To take my example above, the initial thought now becomes "Perhaps I am useful." Now what would your assumption be and how would you behave? Then what might the feedback be? And your new belief about yourself?

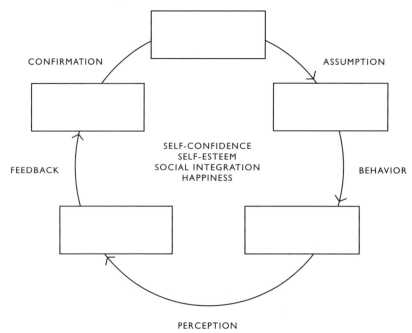

If you worked some other examples on a separate sheet, go back now and rework them from a positive, optimistic standpoint.

Now you need to begin to practice starting from this more positive attitude in every transaction, every day, and see what happens. It will help speed up the process as you also practice some positive thinking every day. Here are some positive thoughts—affirmations— to get you going. Remembering them and saying them to yourself, especially in situations where previously you may have been feeling vulnerable and negative, will have a profound effect not only on your heart chakra and your mind but also on your relationships and your whole life. The best affirmations are the ones you make yourself, so play with them until you feel they are just right for you.

> *I am lovable and people are happy to be with me.*
>
> *Every moment offers me some new gift; I am open to receive these with love and grati-tude.*
>
> *Every transaction with every person offers me opportunity and possibility; I give and receive in love and gratitude.*
>
> *I greet everyone with respect, openness, loving-kindness and compassion.*
>
> *I know that I have unique and wonderful gifts to offer the world; in simply relaxing and being me, I manifest these in the world.*

Now add some of your own:

_____

_____

_____

_____

_____

_____

> *Attachment tends to lead to negative conse-quences whereas love and com-passion lead to positive conse-quences.*
> HIS HOLINESS, THE DALAI LAMA

Exercise Two

You will need:
- ✎ This book and your pen
- ✎ 45 minutes of uninterrupted time

This exercise will help you shift your focus outward to reduce judgment and encompass more of the world and the joy in it.

When our heart chakra is unhappy, pain, grief and negativity make us quite egocentric; we become self-absorbed and lose interest in other people. Shifting our focus from ourselves and opening to share an interest in what others are feeling and doing helps get our plight into perspective and heal our hearts. However this is not an invitation to shift into denial and paper over our difficulties, nor to become codependently involved in other people's lives and rescue them. Doing this exercise with the focus on someone you have some difficulty with is particularly rewarding.

Bring someone you have a problem with to mind and write down their name.

_____

What do you know about them?

_____

_____

_____

_____

_____

_____

_____

_____

> *Love is what keeps your moon in orbit around your planet. Love is what keeps you circling around your sun. Love is food for the soul. Love is what heals.*
>
> ANDREW RAMER

What do you like about them?

_____

_____

_____

_____

What do you dislike about them?

_____

_____

_____

_____

_____

_____

_____

_____

Why do you think they behave as they do?

_____

_____

_____

_____

_____

_____

_____

_____

On what do you base this assumption?

_____

_____

_____

_____

_____

_____

_____

_____

What do you know about the trauma in their life?

_____

_____

_____

_____

_____

_____

_____

Might the trauma in their life be a reason (not an excuse) for how they behave?

_____

What do you think it must feel like to be them and suffer what they suffer? Try for a moment to put yourself in their shoes. What does it feel like?

_____

Could you come any nearer to understanding them with your heart, and forgiving them if necessary?

_____

How does your heart feel? (Forgiveness always has a remarkably healing effect on the heart chakra.)

_____

> _Love is the perfect sum of all delight._
> TOBIAS HUME, 1645

Before you leave this exercise—does that person's behavior reflect anything about your own? (Almost always, the people we like or dislike are reflecting something about us—either something lovely that we need to be proud of, or something we do not like about ourselves, which then needs to be brought to the light of day so it can heal.)

It reminds me of when:

_____

_____

_____

Exercise Three

You will need:
- ∾ This book and a pen
- ∾ Some writing paper and an envelope
- ∾ 30 to 45 minutes of uninterrupted time today, then another 45 minutes three or four days later, and again three or four days after that

Write a letter to yourself as you might to your best friend, telling her/him about your sorrows, worries and frustrations; the things that have hurt you that you still have not healed; your wishes, plans and goals; your achievements and the things you are proud of and that please you. Say what is good in your life and what you would really like to change. Add anything else you wish, then end it appropriately and put it in an envelope, seal it and leave it somewhere safe.

Three or four days later …

Make yourself comfortable in your safe place and close your eyes and breathe. Prepare yourself to be available and lovingly helpful to your best friend. When you are ready, open and read the letter slowly and carefully, with compassion and understanding. Now, from a very loving perspective, write a reply addressing every point, saying how you feel about what has been happening to your friend, comforting where necessary, rejoicing where that is fitting and making suggestions about what needs to be done—perhaps you could make her/him a list. In ending, tell her/him how you value her/him. Leave the letter in a safe place.

Three or four days later …

Open the letter and read the compassionate advice given you by your friend. Let the love touch your heart. Look at what needs to be done and decide where you could start? What one small change could you make today? (There is always something.) Now make a realistic time schedule for making changes.

For example:

- From today I will remember to treat myself as I would treat my best friend; every time I think or say something negative about myself I will change it to something more appropriate and kind.

- Today I will look in the phone book for an exercise class I can join.

- Tomorrow I will buy myself some flowers.

- Next month I will give myself a budget to spend on things important for my well-being and spiritual growth, for example some healing music, some candles, a crystal, some beautiful oil.

- On Friday I will find my old swimming certificate and put it where I can see it and feel proud of my accomplishment.

- Every day I will massage my body with some nice lotion or oil after my bath or shower and book a professional massage when I can.

- The next time my sister calls and says she and her family are coming for the weekend I'll ask for time to think it over to decide whether that is convenient for me.

_____

_____

_____

_____

_____

_____

_____

_____

_____

_____

_____

One can overcome the forces of the negative emotions, like anger or hatred, by cultivating their counterforces, like love and compassion.

HIS HOLINESS, THE
DALAI LAMA

Exercise Four

You will need:

∾ This book and your pen

∾ 30 minutes of uninterrupted time in your safe place

Since I want my mind and spirit to be filled with good and beautiful things, I try to feed it a lovely diet of good news, positive thoughts, healing music, pleasant memories, loving actions, sweet perfumes, gentle touches and uplifting sights. Since I do not want it to be churning over disaster, murder and tragedy, I try not to read about those things or watch them on film or television; I know they exist and am not burying my head in the sand. I can still send out love and healing to victims and perpetrators everywhere and also to those I know are struggling with the painful agendas they have set for themselves in this lifetime.

Let us look at the diet you feed your heart chakra:

Are your heart and mind more troubled than they need to be because of what you feed them? What is your usual spiritual food? (For example, music, love, art, beauty or violent films, gossip, bad news?) What do those soap operas you watch teach you? Do you begin to feel that scheming, lying, cheating and plotting revenge are acceptable ways of being? Honestly now …

_____

_____

_____

_____

_____

Is your spiritual diet good for you? (Perhaps you could ask yourself if you would be willing to put the equivalent in physical terms into your body. What do you think would happen to you if you fed it bad food, poisonous substances and unclean water?)

_____

_____

List twenty ways you could improve your heart chakra diet—I have given you some examples.

1. Each evening make a list of five demonstrations of goodness I have been aware of during the day and add to it by sending thoughts of love and light out to at least five people.

2. Stop renting videos that bring murder into my sitting room.

3. Give hugs and tender strokes where I have permission and it seems appropriate.

4. Do some small act of service every day.

5. Let go of my addiction to soaps.

6. _____

7. _____

8. _____

9. _____

10. _____

11. _____

12. _____

13. _____

14. _____

15. _____

16. _____

17. _____

18. _____

19. _____

20. _____

> *Everyone has talent. What is rare is the courage to follow that talent in the dark place where it leads.*
>
> Erica Jong

Take a deep breath. Make a commitment to incorporate these into your daily life, then congratulate yourself for improving your spiritual health from this moment on.

Meditations

Meditation One

You will need:
- ～ This book and your pen
- ～ Your safe place
- ～ An hour of uninterrupted time

You know the induction by heart now, so go through the usual routine to get relaxed and comfortable.

Remember that anything that may arise is only a memory and that nothing from the past can hurt you now. You have already survived.

This time you are going back to being between 12 and 16, and wrapping together the events, the happenings and the feelings of that time. You have already unearthed them. Take your time …

And now, with a thought, allow light to shine into, around and through that time and all the events and people. Let the light heal everything of that time and in particular the part of you that has remained stuck between the ages of 12 and 16. Let the light, and with it love, shine into every part of you and allow you to heal …

Now with a beam of love from your heart, wrap your young self firmly, comfortably, securely. Hold her/him so that she/he feels safe.

Now, if you are able, send forgiveness to the people and events of that time—send healing to yourself if you are uncomfortable about what you did then. See yourself and all others with compassion and know that everyone, including you, were doing their best. Now release yourself from any connection you no longer want to have. The past is the past and the past can be healed. Everything can be released.

Now … as always, if you feel you are not ready to go on, stop and return very gently to the room, grounding yourself before you open your eyes.

But if you are able, rise to a higher spiritual level and see that the people who did whatever they did then were acting within their own process and from their own pain and turmoil … forgive them … let them go with compassion and understanding.

And now, if you can, rise to an even higher spiritual level and see that these people were in fact teaching you whatever you needed to know in this lifetime in the only way you could learn it. They were a necessary part of your process as you were of theirs. So, if you can, send them gratitude for having taught you and having played an important part in your life, and let them go with compassion and love.

Take your time.

And now all is clear. Breathe love and compassion into that young part of yourself. Wrap yourself in endless love. Let there be peace and healing. Breathe and enjoy the peace. Know that you will never be quite the same again since you are healed of the past and your heart is at peace at last.

Now, take your time. When you are ready, gently return to the room. Take a deep breath and fill your physical body with oxygen. Become aware again of your physical presence. Move your toes and fingers. Put your arms around your body and love it …

Enjoy …

When you are ready, come back to behind your closed eyes. And when you are truly here, get well-grounded … and gently open your eyes.

Take your time … have a drink of water … stretch a little. Then enter whatever you wish in your journal. Take a break if you wish, before going on to the final heart meditation.

Meditation Two

You will need:

⌁ This book and your pen

⌁ Your safe place

⌁ An hour of uninterrupted time

Now, close your eyes. Return once again to your safe place within yourself. Take your focus down to the level of your heart. Allow yourself to see a beautiful pink rosebud there. Its petals are closed. See it in its as yet unformed beauty. Gently observe it, and when you are

Joy is the source that allows for transformation. Joy is what blesses. Joy is your true self.
ANDREW RAMER

ready, breathe warmth and light into it and watch it begin to open. Softly, the petals start to move, slipping over each other, opening the bloom. Opening and opening to its full beauty. A wonderful, fully formed pink rose. Now it is at its peak, a spectacular bloom in all its glory. Though all of its stages of development were lovely, now at its fullest blooming it achieves perfection—the fully formed magnificent flower.

See this rose as the metaphor for your own blossoming. Now you are achieving your full bloom. You are at the peak of your blooming—you are, like the rose, fully opened, fully formed, stunning, beautiful, magnificent … This rose is your gift to yourself. You and your full flowering are a gift to the world. Hold the beauty … hold the magnificence. You are the gift. Let yourself enjoy the feelings … let yourself savor the moment. Let yourself embrace the magnificence of your maturity, your full flowering. Enjoy …

Now, from the center of the rose, allow a beam of love to go out to wherever you wish —healing, cleansing, purest love. Notice that as you send it out, you are healed by it also. Let it shine wherever it is needed most … let it heal wherever it falls. Let this unconditional love heal the world. Let this unconditional love be your neverending gift to the world.

Stay as long as you wish. When you are ready, allow the beam of love to gently cease—though it will heal you forever. Let yourself hold onto the rose, enclosing it in your heart.

Smile … feel yourself healing. Enjoy.

Take your time. When you are ready gently bring your focus back to your physical body. Be aware of your weight on the floor. Allow yourself to be well grounded, in touch with the earth. Gently begin to stretch and be totally aware, returning your mind to the room. Make sure you are back to that place behind your eyes. Feel your physical body. Put your arms around it … hold it … love it.

When you are ready, very gently open your eyes. Take your time. Just be.

Affirmations

My heart is filed with love for all the universe.
Loving energy flows through me and fills me.
I open to loving, mutually supportive, trusting, respectful relationships.

Make your own affirmations

_____

_____

_____

_____

_____

> *Our loving is a work in progress. We are continuously refining it, honing it, adding to it, shaping it. That is what we think we are doing. We also know that love is continuously refining, honing, adding to and shaping us.*
>
> PETER
> MCWILLIAMS

Notes

> *By bringing about a change in our outlook towards things and events, all phenomena can become a source of happiness.*
>
> HIS HOLINESS, THE DALAI LAMA

CHAPTER FIVE

The Throat Chakra

❧

Let there be many windows in your soul,
That all the glory of the Universe may beautify it.
Not the narrow pane of one poor creed can catch the radiant rays
That shine from countless sources.
Tear away the blinds of superstition;
Let the light pour through fair windows,
Broad as truth itself
And high as heaven.
Tune your ear to all the worldless music of the stars
And to the voice of nature,
And your heart shall turn to truth and goodness as the plant turns to the sun.
A thousand unseen hands reach down to help you
to their peace-crowned heights,
And all the forces of the firmament shall fortify your strength.
Be not afraid to thrust aside half-truths and grasp the whole.

RALPH WALDO TRINE

From basic instincts and survival at our root chakra, through the sacral with its accent on sexuality, balance, flexibility and flow, we came to power at the solar plexus and love at the heart. Now we come to communicating our truth, our integrity and our unique message to the world.

What You Can Hope to Gain by Working with Your Throat Chakra

- To communicate articulately, with power and clarity
- Discovery of your own unique truth as you open to understand more of the universal truth
- A better understanding of your unique integrity
- A reduction in judgment as you understand the true meaning of integrity
- Verbal expression that allows you to share who you are with the outside world
- Discovery of your vocation

Now, take a look at the following questions and assess for yourself the work you need to do here.

SELF-ASSESSMENT QUESTIONNAIRE

☐ 1. Do you have difficulty expressing your feelings verbally?

☐ 2. Do you sometimes fail to choose your words with care and blurt out something you did not mean to say?

☐ 3. Is your creativity blocked?

☐ 4. Do you have problems with rhythm in your life—either externally, being unable to feel the beat of music, or internally, with rhythmical functions such as heartbeat, breathing or menstrual cycle?

☐ 5. Have you ever had a thyroid problem?

☐ 6. Do you have difficulty with your hearing or speech?

☐ 7. Have you had dental problems, or trouble with your neck or ears, nose and throat?

☐ 8. Did you have trauma or problems between 16 and 21?

☐ 9. Do you find it difficult to pick up social cues—for example when someone wants to speak, or when they are finished speaking and it is your turn?

☐ 10. Do you interrupt, or have parallel conversations with people rather than an easy dialogue?

☐ 11. Do you sometimes find yourself with little if anything to say, then at other times pour out torrents of words with little meaning?

☐ 12. Do you have difficulty deciding for yourself what is right and wrong, and instead follow other people's ethics or none at all?

☐ 13. Do you wander from job to job thinking every time that this might be the one you really love?

☐ 14. Do you tell lies or exaggerate the truth to make it seem better?

☐ 15. Do you take yourself and life very seriously, failing to take time to play and have fun?

If you answer "yes" to most of the above, then you probably have problems with your throat chakra. Now let us learn more about it so you can start to heal it.

∽ BASICS OF THE THROAT CHAKRA ∽

SITE: Though it shines out horizontally at the front of the throat, unlike the other chakras, the angle is slightly raised at the back of the body.

COLOR: The throat chakra rotates at the speed of clear, bright blue or turquoise light.

ACTIVATION AND DEVELOPMENT: This chakra begins developing at about 16 and continues until 21, though as with all the chakras, its maturation continues throughout life. It comes back into focus between 46 and 51 and again between 76 and 81.

SPECIAL CONNECTIONS: This chakra is associated with the sacral chakra, manifesting the creativity that begins there.

ASSOCIATED SENSE: It governs the senses of hearing and speech, including self-expression.

GLANDULAR ASSOCIATION: The thyroid and parathyroid glands—the thyroid gland covers aspects of growth, temperature control, energy production and carbohydrate and fat metabolism, and also intellectual development in children. The parathyroid glands are concerned with calcium metabolism.

NEUROLOGICAL CONNECTION: It is connected with the pharyngeal plexus, which supplies the throat, pharynx, tongue, palate and also the brachial plexus, which supplies the arm.

ASSOCIATED AURIC BODY: It is associated with the fifth layer of the aura, the etheric template (sometimes called the ketheric body), which always holds a perfect template of the physical body, even if we have trauma or surgery that results in us losing part of our physical body.

VERBAL EXPRESSION: Our thoughts and ideas, once shared with the world through communication and conversation, not only help us reveal who we are, but also simultaneously invite into our world all those who hear us. Everyone is rewarded by the exchange.

HEARING AND LISTENING: Active and attentive listening completes the loop of good communication, allowing us to hear all that is said, every nuance, pause and verbal punctuation, adding to our appreciation of the message.

NON-VERBAL COMMUNICATION: Understanding is further enhanced by signals we receive from the movements and mannerisms of others. Sometimes the non-verbal communication—body language—tells us more than the words being spoken.

INTERNAL COMMUNICATION: We also communicate internally, listening to our body and the signals it constantly gives us; our soul as it gently guides us; our mind with its constant chatter; and the Universe, its higher wisdom everpresent as a constant backdrop.

WIT, HUMOR AND IMPROVISATION: Though to some extent wit and humor are part of personality, it is the well-developed throat chakra that links feelings, thoughts, intuitions and impressions and allows us to express them spontaneously with wit and humor.

TRUTH AND THE ABILITY AND WILLINGNESS TO UPDATE IT: Though the whole universal truth is available to us all simultaneously and constantly, how much of it we are consciously aware of depends on our development and experience. Thus, our understanding of the truth is not static fact, but a living, constantly changing and developing dynamic process. Hopefully we have courage to express the truth, as we know it, even though it may invalidate what we previously believed.

INTEGRITY AND MORALITY: Integrity is a function of the truth as we know it and our emotional and mental state and individual circumstances. Thus our integrity is highly personal—I might allow myself to do something that you would consider unacceptable, and vice versa. Morality changes over time—what we did quite happily in our teens or twenties we may not consider moral now. Behaving in a manner that threatens our integrity and morality costs us in guilt, shame, regret and sorrow.

CREATIVITY: Ideas that emerged at the sacral chakra are elaborated here. Whatever our unique gifts, the throat chakra, with the help of the healthy brow chakra, helps us have courage to manifest them and share them with the world.

VOCATION: Though our hearts tend to lead us in the direction we need to go, and our brow chakra adds intuition, it is the throat chakra that brings together truth, integrity, creativity and communication and makes our passionate and purposeful vocation a reality.

CLAIRAUDIENCE: This is the gift of inner hearing without an external stimulus, which we may perceive more as a knowing that appears to come from nowhere but that we "hear." Even those who are deaf can develop clairaudience.

CHANNELING AND MEDIUMSHIP: In the last 30 or 40 years the quality of the ancient gift of channeling has changed, and many people have opened to communicate with beings on the higher soul planes and access, in language we understand, wisdom and teaching about almost any subject. Mediumship facilitates communication with the souls of those who have lived on Earth fairly recently.

TELEPATHY: The throat and brow chakras working in unison allow for the transmission or receipt of information directly, without the stimulus of speech or physical hearing. We are all capable of telepathy to some extent, particularly with people we love or with whom we feel in tune. Many mothers tune in to their children; lovers often know what the other is thinking; or we intend to call someone when they call us.

PHYSICAL ASSOCIATIONS: The throat chakra governs the neck and shoulders and the lower part of the face, up to but not including the eyes—including the ears, nose and throat, teeth, tongue and cervical spine, vocal cords and thyroid and parathyroid glands. The trachea and esophagus have associations here and also with the heart chakra and solar plexus respectively.

❧ AND IF THINGS GO WRONG ... ❧

If there has been trauma at the time of its development or injury later involving the site of the throat chakra, in adulthood you may have some of the following difficulties.

POOR COMMUNICATION: All aspects of communication may be hampered—speech (which of course reflects thinking) with its clarity, syntax, tone and volume; listening and truly hearing all that is being said; attention that helps us really hear the message under the words. Often contradiction between our verbal and non-verbal signals confuses those who try to communicate with us.

UNWILLINGNESS TO UPDATE THE TRUTH: We remain stubbornly fixed in old ideas, beliefs and "truths" since we are unable or unwilling to integrate the new information that is constantly being made available to us.

TELLING LIES: Acknowledgment of the truth and also the courage to tell it are challenging. Lying becomes an easy option and eventually a habit. Exaggeration and embroidering the truth for effect are really lying.

POOR SENSE OF HUMOR: Being witty, funny and appreciating others' humor is lost to us and we miss out on much of the fun in life.

TAKING OURSELVES TOO SERIOUSLY: Lack of playfulness and lightness and the ability to laugh at ourselves and life (not other people!) makes us take both ourselves and life very seriously, and we become intense and difficult to be with. Sadly, we ourselves then often become the butt of other peoples' jokes.

BLOCKED CREATIVITY: Throat chakra problems block our creativity, and with a paucity of ideas or dreams to manifest we find ourselves living in a seemingly colorless world where everyone else appears to be having a party! What's more, we often feel that this bland world is the real one, and we therefore fail to strive to change it.

DIFFICULTIES IN FINDING THE RIGHT CAREER OR VOCATION: Job after job may seem promising initially but rarely develops into something fulfilling and worthwhile. Purpose and vocation can hardly be conceptualized.

LIVING AN AMORAL LIFE: Developing a system of ethics based on personal integrity is difficult and we may live an amoral life or else abide by a rigid moral code that we have adopted rather than shaped on our own principles.

PHYSICAL SYMPTOMS: Recurrent sore throats, colds, swollen glands, neck and shoulder pain and dental problems abound. There may also be symptoms of hypo—or hyperthyroidism. The former presents with lethargy, weight gain, low mood, coarsening of skin and hair, and the latter with weight loss, anxiety, poor sleep and increased energy accompanied by jitteriness and agitation.

Oils and Gemstones for the Throat Chakra

Lavender and hyacinth oils are gently soothing, while patchouli and white musk will help stimulate creativity. Turquoise helps improve communication, creative expression and emotional balance and also deepens meditation and clarifies intuition. It is also said to bring good luck and prosperity, and also to preserve love and friendship. Fluorite helps us stand up for justice and speak out with integrity against oppression, while stimulating our creative capacity and learning skills, thus helping us fulfill our potential. Blue lace agate helps us remain centered and calm while aquamarine helps us think more clearly, reduce stress and improve creativity. Lapis lazuli strengthens the thyroid and also augments psychic abilities while inspiring greater creative expression and improving vitality. Silver is renowned for improving speech and strengthening faith in your higher self, so if you have some silver jewelry with any of these stones, it would be good to wear.

Now You

Now let us bring to light what needs to be healed—so whether your memories are wonderful or filled with pain, please record them here.

Breathe. Take a few deep breaths and record what comes to mind when you focus on these times in your life. It is unlikely that you are doing this work at the time of the third focus, but I have included it here just in case!

What I remember of the time between 16 and 21 is:

_____

_____

_____

_____

_____

_____

_____

_____

_____

Important people of that time include (these may be family members, teachers, friends, people who loved you or people who may have hurt you):

_____   _____

_____   _____

_____   _____

_____   _____

My feelings about this time and the people are:

_____

_____

_____

_____

_____

_____

_____

_____

_____

_____

Second Focus

What was happening in my life between ages 46 and 51:

_____

_____

_____

_____

_____

_____

_____

_____

> *There are two ways to live your life. One is as though nothing is a miracle. The other is as though everything is a miracle.*
>
> ALBERT EINSTEIN

The major people in my life were:

_____   _____

_____   _____

_____   _____

My feelings about this time and the people are:

_____

_____

_____

_____

_____

_____

_____

_____

_____

Don't be afraid to take a big step if one is indicated. You can't cross a chasm in two small jumps.
DAVID LLOYD
GEORGE

Third Focus

What is happening in my life between ages 76 and 81:

_____

_____

_____

_____

_____

_____

_____

_____

_____

The major people in my life are:

_____   _____

_____   _____

_____   _____

_____   _____

My feelings about this time and the people are:

_____

_____

_____

_____

_____

_____

_____

_____

_____

_____

What All This Gave Me

List here the *positive* effects on your life—for example: I had to learn to stand up for myself; I had to learn to confront issues; I got into starting to heal myself; I got so sick that I had to get help. If you cannot see them now, just skip this section and return to it when it all makes more sense. When you do that, please do both of the meditations again as your capacity to forgive, heal and come to inner peace will have increased significantly.

_____

_____

_____

_____

_____

_____

_____

So now that you have your throat chakra and its problems in mind, let us go on to heal it.

Exercises

These exercises will help you overcome the pain of the past both emotionally and physically, and also flow into a balanced, harmonious future.

Exercise One

You will need:
- ❧ This book and your pen
- ❧ Hopefully some extra paper
- ❧ 30 minutes today and then a little time every morning when you wake and every evening before you go to sleep
- ❧ Your schedule or appointment book

Living in a state of gratitude completely changes our lives, as we begin to see the gifts and the joy in everything. However, gratitude needs to be verbalized regularly—whether to your partner, friends, colleagues or the Divine. Appreciation of people's gifts and friendship and simply their presence in your life will help heal you and them. Inner thanksgiving is fine, and there are times when a silent prayer is proper; however, you can open your heart and your throat and give gratitude at any time. Even if your gratitude is written, either in your journal or in letters, you set up a new vibration in your life.

What are you grateful for today? List at least five things.

1. _____
2. _____
3. _____
4. _____
5. _____

(Continue on a spare sheet of paper if you wish—as you do this daily, your list will grow and grow.)

Who do you need to tell that you are grateful?

_____

_____

_____

_____

_____

_____

_____

How are you going to do that? (For example, write a letter to my mother; make a phone call to my friend; send a silent prayer out into the world.)

_____

_____

_____

_____

_____

_____

> *A clay pot sitting in the sun will always be a clay pot. It has to go through the white heat of the furnace to become porcelain.*
>
> MILDRED WHITE-STOUVEN

Now set dates to do all of those things—today would be great!—and transfer them into your appointment book.

Finally, make a commitment that you will spend a few minutes morning and evening bringing to mind what you are grateful for, whether it is that the rain will make the flowers grow, or that the person who cut you off on the way home actually made you think of how you sometimes drive, or that people in your life are wonderful, that someone smiled and made your day. Every single word and deed has a gift within it for which we can be grateful once we start to be more aware. Enjoy setting yourself the challenge of reframing everything to the positive. For example, the person who spoke sharply to me made me think how often I do that and how others may feel. I will be conscious now not to do that. Often the things we do not like are the ones giving us opportunities to bring something of ourselves to the light—now is that not a great gift?

Exercise Two

You will need:
- ⌒ This book and a pen
- ⌒ At least an hour of uninterrupted time to assess your home
- ⌒ Later, some time to make changes
- ⌒ 30 minutes to make a list of what you need
- ⌒ Half a day to put it all into practice

Though this exercise is aimed at your outward space, bear in mind that everything is an extension of everything else, so where we are, how we live and what is happening on the outside has a profound effect on every part of our being. Here you are going to clear your space with sound, which will help clear your inner space too, bringing healing, increasing creativity, nurturing your sense of hearing and enhancing your communication skills, since it clears your throat chakra. I suggest you start with your living space, then when you feel ready, extend outward—once you have cleared inside your home, you might like to look at where you could add beautiful sound to the outside—wind chimes, plants that rustle in the wind, something to encourage birds into your garden, etc. However, be aware that others share your space outside and loud noises may not be to their taste. Do not forget your work-space, being aware that here too, others may not share your tastes—a good time to practice some good communication and negotiating skills!

You can create your own sound, of course, by singing, clapping your hands, chanting, beating a drum, using a singing bowl. Whatever you choose, I think you will be surprised at the difference it makes to the energy in your space, and indeed your own personal energy. Try it!

First of all, go from room to room and clear any clutter—if you have not done this for some time, just take it easy. Clearing too much at once will simply upset the balance of energy you are used to and make you feel strange. One room at a time, or even a single cupboard will do for a start, but then make a date with yourself to do the next bit. When the clutter is cleared, then you will to use the power of sound to clarify the energy and make your home feel wonderful.

List here the sounds that are particularly pleasing to you. (For example, the human voice, birdsong, music—I swoon at saxophones and drums!—bells, wind chimes, the sound of the wind, thunder, running water, rain, singing bowls—these are all favorites of mine.)

_____

_____

_____

_____

_____

_____

Where could you place these in your home? (Walk through your home making notes on one room at a time)

_____

_____

_____

_____

_____

_____

> *We will discover the nature of our own particular genius when we stop trying to conform to our own or other people's models. Learn to be ourselves and allow our natural channels to open.*
>
> TAOS GAWAIN

If you play safe in life, you have decided that you don't want to grow.
SHIRLEY
HUPSTEDLER

Now make a date to collect what you need and place it around your home. You could, of course, start with just opening the windows and playing some music (not too loud—remember your neighbors!) or go around your home clapping your hands—do not forget the corners and behind furniture, waking up the energy and moving out the cobwebs.

Finally walk around and sit in various chairs to feel the energy you have created. Enjoy!

Exercise Three

This is a two-part exercise. For the first part, you will need:

❧ At least an hour to browse in a music shop

❧ This book and a pen

For the second part, you will need:

❧ An hour of uninterrupted time in your safe place

❧ This book and a pen

❧ Extra sheets of paper

❧ A music system

Music is the most mind-altering substance known to humans, and it is legal. Whatever your taste or your mood; whether you choose an earthy, grounding piece for the root chakra, a flowing piece that tunes into the water element of the sacral, a powerful stirring epic for the solar plexus or something gentle and loving for the heart, all of them are perceived here at the throat chakra. Music for healing—that you can get both lost and found in—may be different from the music you play in your car or dance to at a party. However, adding some movement is good for you on many levels, so perhaps you could include some dance music too. You may already have your favorites, but if not, please go and browse in your music shop and find what lifts you into a healing space. Some of my favorites are listed in *The 7 Healing Chakras*.

_____

_____

_____

List your favorites here. Try to list at least one piece for each chakra.

_____

_____

_____

_____

_____

_____

_____

Peace is not the absence of anything. Peace is creative, dynamic, alive. Peace is what fills the spaces in the universe. Peace is day to love's night. Peace is active, vital, engaging. Peace is the fire of the sun, lighting and warming. Peace is the sunflower you cultivate in the garden of your life. Peace is pursuing your dreams for yourself and for all the earth.

ANDREW RAME

Now, take some time for yourself, take the phone off the hook and settle yourself comfortably in your safe place. Have your music system available and the track you are going to use ready so you can switch it on easily without moving around too much. For this exercise either sit or lie, whichever you prefer. Close your eyes. Take a few deep breaths, imagine a beautiful sky blue flower at your throat and watch its petals open. Switch on your music and just allow the sound to take you wherever you need to go. You need not actively listen unless you want to. Just be in the sound. Let it flow into you through your open throat chakra. Be part of it. Feel the power of it.

Allow the music to completely finish before you move. Now, just let whatever is in your mind empty itself onto the next page. Use some extra paper, if necessary. Do not worry about the grammar, spelling or about it making sense. Just let your hand keep moving and pour out whatever you have to communicate. Try not to think, just let it flow and appear on the page. When it feels complete, just spend a moment sitting or lying, allowing yourself to heal. Make sure you are well-grounded before you resume your daily tasks.

_____

_____

_____

_____

_____

_____

_____

_____

_____

_____

_____

_____

_____

_____

_____

_____

_____

_____

_____

> *... and then the day came when the risk to remain tight in a bud was more painful than the risk it took to blossom.*
>
> ANAÏS NIN

Exercise Four

You will need:

- ∿ 45 minutes of uninterrupted time
- ∿ Your sacred space or some other place where you feel comfortable to make your own sound

This exercise encourages you to use your own voice as a healing tool for yourself, in that you will be clarifying and healing your throat chakra and benefiting every aspect of your life, and also the whole universe, since the vibrations you radiate now will go on forever touching everything.

Chanting is the art of saying or singing words or sounds repeatedly as part of sacred practice and is effective for enhancing awareness and focusing concentration as an aid to meditation. There are ancient chants and invocations you could use, or you can make your own with whatever words or sounds you wish. Chanting your own name is very powerful. Begin quietly, then alter the tone, power and texture of your voice, noticing what a difference that makes. Often, a flood of self-love and self-esteem is released by doing this simple but powerful exercise.

The word "Om" is powerful as a chant, a mantra or to sound your own note.

Now close your eyes, focus on any of your chakras for a few moments, then fill your lungs with air and allow your throat to open. Simply let any note that feels comfortable be released through your throat. Do not worry about what it sounds like. Sound this note several times as your throat starts to clear. Now start to play with changing its quality and texture—you can sing it with gentleness and sweetness and then with power and force. Note the energy in your body and in the space around you as it changes according to the vibration of the sound waves you are creating. Feel the vibration in your cells, in your muscles, in your organs.

Now choose a different chakra and repeat the process. Instinctively the note you sound will be different. Enjoy sounding this chakra and notice the different vibrations in your body and around you.

Focus on each chakra in turn, sounding each one.

Now draw the energy of all of your chakras to your throat. With the power of them all at once, open your throat and sound the note of your soul. Sound it with sweetness and gentleness and then with power. Note again any physical sensations.

Take another breath and sound your soul's tone again, holding it for as long as you can. Note how the power of it increases as your throat chakra clears and the healing vibrations touch every cell and extend through your aura and out into the Universe. Let the Universe hear you now. In this single sound, extend your truth and integrity to the world.

_____

_____

_____

_____

_____

_____

_____

> *Communication is the response you get. ... if you don't get the response you want, you haven't communicated properly.*
>
> ONE MINUTE
> MILLIONAIRE

Meditations

Meditation One

You will need:
☙ This book and your pen
☙ 45 minutes of uninterrupted time in your safe place

☙ ☙ ☙

As usual, get comfortable, focus on your breathing and then let go of anything negative. When you are relaxed, take your focus back to the ages of 16 to 21. Now send love and light from your heart and wrap it around your self of that time. Hold and protect your self tenderly ... gently. Hold securely and with love, just as you needed to be held then.

You have already unearthed the detail of this time, so now bring together this time and the events and people, ready to let yourself be healed. And if you are able, send light and forgiveness to cleanse and heal that time.

Now move to a higher spiritual level. Perhaps you can see that the people who did whatever they did then, including you, did so because of their own process and where they were in their lives at that time. They were living through their own damage and pain. If you can understand that, send them forgiveness with compassion. Free yourself and them once and for all and let them go.

And now, if you are able, move into the third phase and raise yourself to yet a higher spiritual level and look again. Maybe now you can see that those who were part of your life then were teaching you lessons necessary for your growth. They were helping you be more complete as you were simultaneously helping them. Now, if you can, send forgiveness with love, compassion and gratitude to them and to yourself and set yourself free. Let them go and let the past be healed.

When you are ready, give thanks. Now allow your young self to be integrated again with a sense of peace and wholeness.

Stay for as long as you wish, then, when you are ready, become more aware of your physical being. Feel your fingers and toes and move them. Have a gentle stretch. When you feel fully aware at that place behind your closed eyes, take a deep breath and fill your cells with oxygen. Send gratitude to the highest possible place, and when you are ready, open your eyes.

Have a drink of water and record whatever you wish.

_____

_____

_____

_____

_____

_____

> *May it be the real I who speaks. May it be real Thou that I speak to.*
> C.S. Lewis

Meditation Two

You will need:

❧ This book and a pen

❧ 45 minutes of uninterrupted time

Use the usual method to get relaxed and let go of anything negative.

Now, gently take your focus down to your throat, to the front of your neck. With your eyes closed, visualize that area. See there a beautiful blue or turquoise light.

See that light shining out into the distance, radiating in all directions. It is sending light to the world, offering love and communication equally to the souls of all others. Like a searchlight, it is clearing paths of communication.

Now, down this wonderful path of light, send out loving messages to the world. If you wish, focus lovingly on particular individuals, and as you send out this wonderful healing light, have the conviction that every good intention of this moment of clarity will be received.

In absolute clarity and with love, send out messages as you telepathically communicate with the whole universe. Extend your focus out beyond yourself, out beyond the planet, across the horizons of time and space to share your love, to share healing, to improve communication, to promote good everywhere for all people. Let this powerful message of love and gratitude and desire for communication with all clear your true path.

Now, allow any information that is for your higher good to enter into your throat chakra via this beautiful path of blue light—wisdom about your vocation, your way forward, your ultimate truth. Let the information simply flow in. Trust that what you will receive will be absolutely pure and for your higher good, and relax into being a passive recipient. You need neither think nor try to make it happen.

Now, switch on your tape recorder or pick up your book and pen. Without self-consciousness, open your throat and speak your message. Let it flow without interruption as you capture forever the wisdom you are receiving now.

Continue until you feel it is complete, then close your eyes again and relax. With a single thought, allow all your chakras to open. Draw together the stability and security of your root chakra, the flexibility and balance of your sacral, the power and potential of your solar plexus and the love and compassion of your heart. Now add the vision and understanding of your brow chakra and the divine connection of your crown and allow them all to combine with the truth and integrity of your throat.

Now, open your throat and allow the whole power of your being to issue forth on a single note. Let it flow on a breath. Hold it as long as you can, then take another deep breath and again let the voice of your soul be heard. Let your vibration reach out to the farthest corners of the universe. Know that as your sound moves out into the world everything is changed by it. Let the love you send with it touch the whole world.

For as long as you wish, share your love and this wonderful, healing vibration with the world, and eventually, when the sound ceases, be confident that the healing reverberation will go on forever.

If there are any questions you would like to ask of the Universe, perhaps about your vocation or your mission in life, ask them now and then be silent in your space and allow the voice of the universe to speak to you in love and wisdom. Let its message be incorporated into every part of your being.

Stay as long as you wish, and before you begin your return, give thanks. Then, with a single thought, allow your chakras to close to where they are safe and comfortable.

Take a deep breath, and begin to be aware of your physical presence. Feel your fingers and toes and move them gently. Have a stretch, and when you feel fully aware and well-grounded, gently open your eyes and return to the room.

❧ ❧ ❧

Have a drink of water and record anything you wish in your journal or below.

_____

_____

_____

_____

_____

_____

> *The important thing is this: to be able at a moment's notice to sacrifice what we are for what we could become.*
> CHARLES DU BOIS

_____

_____

_____

Affirmations

I open with clarity and love to share my truth and integrity with the world.

I clarify my voice so that I may share myself with the world in open communication.

With lightness, playfulness, humor and wit, I raise my vibration in the world.

I am open to move along the path of my vocation and welcome all those who are to help me in creating my vision of truth.

Make your own affirmations

_____

_____

_____

_____

_____

_____

Notes

_____

_____

_____

_____

_____

_____

_____

He is made one with Nature; there is heard His voice in all her music; from the moan of thunder to the song of the night's sweet bird.

ADONIS SCHELLING, 1775–1854

> *If any person is compassionate and altruistic, wherever that person moves, he or she will immediately make friends.*
>
> HIS HOLINESS, THE
> DALAI LAMA

_____

_____

_____

_____

_____

_____

_____

_____

_____

_____

_____

_____

_____

_____

_____

_____

_____

_____

_____

_____

_____

_____

_____

_____

_____

_____

_____

_____

CHAPTER SIX

The Brow Chakra

Our deepest fear is not that we are inadequate. Our deepest fear is that we are powerful beyond measure. It is our light, not our darkness that most frightens us.

We ask ourselves, who am I to be brilliant, gorgeous, talented and fabulous? Actually, who are you not to be?

You are a child of God. Your playing small doesn't benefit the world. There's nothing enlightened about shrinking so that other people won't feel insecure around you.

We were born to make manifest the glory of God that is within us. It's not just in some of us, it's in everyone!

And as we let our light shine, we unconsciously give other people the permission to do the same. As we are liberated from our own fear, our presence automatically liberates others.

NELSON MANDELA—INAUGURAL SPEECH, 1994

This is the chakra of command—command of our life, our learning and our dreams. It is the chakra of visualizing what we really desire and—with wisdom, inspiration, insight, perception and understanding—manifesting what is for our higher good.

What You Can Hope to Gain by Working with Your Brow Chakra

- Honing of your intuition so it becomes a constant, amazing tool
- Understanding and wisdom to add to your other gifts
- The ability to visualize what you want and manifest it
- Greater vision of your purpose in the world
- Improved health in your ears, nose, throat and neck
- More insight, with possibly the development of clairvoyance

Now, why not look at the following questions and assess for yourself the work you need to do here.

SELF-ASSESSMENT QUESTIONNAIRE

☐ 1. Do you find it difficult to follow through with ideas and plan your life?

☐ 2. Do you ridicule other people's beliefs, especially in the area of religion and spirituality?

☐ 3. Do you need to find people to blame for various aspects of your life?

☐ 4. Do you have a problem with visualization?

☐ 5. Do you have nightmares?

☐ 6. Is your sleep disturbed?

☐ 7. Do you enjoy putting other people down?

☐ 8. Do you have problems with eyestrain or conjunctivitis?

☐ 9. Do people around you get frustrated with your broken promises?

☐ 10. Do you make commitments but fail to keep them?

☐ 11. Do you suffer from migraines?

☐ 12. Do you have difficulty recognizing and connecting with a power higher than yourself?

☐ 13. Did you have difficulties between the ages of 21 and 26?

☐ 14. Do you have problems with imagination, and need instead to intellectualize everything?

☐ 15. Is intuition something you either ridicule or see as a special gift for other people but not for you?

If you answer "yes" to most of the above, then you probably have problems with your brow chakra. Let us learn more about it so you can start to heal it.

⁓ BASICS OF THE BROW CHAKRA ⁓

SITE: The brow chakra is above and between the eyes, in the midline at the front of your head and at the same level at the back.

COLOR: It is deep indigo blue or purple.

ACTIVATION & DEVELOPMENT: Classically this chakra may begin its development between 21 and 26, though many of us do not spontaneously develop our brow until the time of the second or third focus (51–56 and 81–86 respectively). Some never develop it in this lifetime. Occasionally there is precocious development in actively psychic young people.

SPECIAL CONNECTIONS: It has a special connection with the solar plexus, from which it picks up raw gut feelings and hones them to perfect intuition.

ASSOCIATED SENSE: It is associated with the sense of vision.

GLANDULAR ASSOCIATION: The pineal gland secretes melatonin, which has several functions, including promoting sleep, regulating our body clock and daily biorhythms, supporting libido and possibly preventing aging.

NEUROLOGICAL CONNECTION: Neurologically it is connected with the carotid plexus, supplying the head, neck and ears.

ASSOCIATED AURIC BODY: The celestial body appears as rays of pastel-colored light extending from the body some 48 to 60 inches.

VISION, INSIGHT AND PERCEPTION: Though the brow chakra covers the anatomical and physiological pathways of physical sight, it is also the place for inner vision and insight. As our perception clarifies, we can also create visions for ourselves, our way forward and indeed for the whole world.

～ FUNCTIONS OF THE BROW CHAKRA ～

INSPIRATION AND DEVOTION: On our ascent through our chakras, we become more aware of our connection with the Divine. Devotion deepens and inspiration becomes our natural state. There is a new reverence not only in meditation or prayer, but also in all life, as we become more aware of the constant loving guidance of the great, unseen powers of the universe. We may find ourselves awash with ideas, energy, wisdom and knowledge, or transfixed, held in love and peace.

INTUITION: Here the raw gut feelings of the solar plexus are refined and honed to perfection as we finally take command of the wonderful gift of intuition. Now we can dip into the ocean of universal truth at will and interpret signs from the universe that previously may have gone unnoticed.

PSYCHISM: Being "psychic" is simply an elaboration of intuition, a gift we are all endowed with. The solutions to all problems and answers to all questions are available to us, and, with a little courage and minimal training, we can start to use our psychic skills to tap into previously unrecognized universal wisdom. At this level, hopefully we have the in-

tegrity to treat our gift and what it reveals ethically and with respect and reverence, so as not to abuse anyone's privacy.

WISDOM: Blessed with the combined wisdom of all our previous experiences, we now have access to wisdom beyond teaching, intellectualism or academic learning.

CLAIRVOYANCE: This spiritual gift—seeing without a physical stimulus—allows us to see clearly beyond the horizons of time and space. Anyone can learn to use clairvoyance to some degree, given time and the will to work on it.

LIGHT AND COLOR: Now we perceive light and color as healing and balancing energies that we can utilize for our healing and to enhance our reality.

MAGIC, MIRACLES AND MANIFESTATION: As we develop or heal our brow chakra, we begin to project powerful and wonderful images into the world, eventually manifesting them as our reality. As we improve our skill, almost with a thought, we may manifest what is for our higher good and the higher good of all.

HEALING: Though the capacity to channel healing energy requires a healthy heart chakra and crown chakra, here our ability to fully utilize this gift multiplies. Energy follows intention, and now, with a thought and a vision for the higher good of others, we can send out powerful healing to the farthest corners of the planet.

MIND MESSAGES: This is a further development of telepathy, to actively send loving and healing thoughts across the ether, setting up vibrations that eventually touch the recipient, who will suddenly think of us and possibly return the message with a loving smile. Someone with a healthy brow chakra would never send negative thoughts!

PHYSICAL ASSOCIATIONS: The brow chakra governs the eyes, visual pathways and the head. Though the throat chakra governs the neck and ears, these are also partly touched by the brow chakra.

～ AND IF THINGS GO WRONG ... ～

The brow chakra can function quite well in some aspects even if under-developed or blocked. However, even intellectual brilliance can be improved by the addition of wisdom, self-awareness and the ability to transcend rational thought. Remember that its development may be naturally delayed until much later in life.

INABILITY TO FOLLOW THROUGH WITH CREATIVE IDEAS: Though creativity is a function of both the sacral and the throat chakras, if we have a block or lack of development at the brow, our good ideas are never quite followed through, and we become surrounded by plans that never quite came to completion, promises we did not keep, commitments we failed to honor and lots of frustrated people!

BLAMING OTHERS FOR OUR OWN SHORTCOMINGS: Lacking the clarity to

see that we have created the mess we find ourselves in, we project our own frustration and blame others for the fact that our lives clogged with half-fulfilled plans.

STUNTED VISION: Though we might perform well in a restricted, controlled environment where we can assume a great degree of control, we are rarely able to open to a greater vision, and instead plagiarize others' ideas.

RIDICULE: Since unlimited joy eludes us, and the mystical is beyond us, we are inclined to reduce everything to the material and demand proof, while ridiculing those who can experience the wonder of the spiritual, dismissing them as delusional and prone to flights of fancy.

PUTTING OTHERS DOWN: Ridicule, insensitivity and sheer disbelief lead us to cruelly put others down, trampling on the finer emo-

tions of those who are open to seeing things differently. Sometimes we seem bent on trying to prove that our negative view of the world is correct.

PHYSICAL SYMPTOMS: In this chakra more than any other, there may be little if any physical manifestation of the problem, though sometimes nightmares or epilepsy may give a clue. Vision may be affected, along with symptoms such as eyestrain and conjunctivitis. Headaches and migraine may occur and there may be difficulties with memory. Since the pineal gland secretes melatonin, which stimulates sleep, there may be sleeping difficulties.

Oils and Gemstones for the Brow Chakra

Violet, rose and geranium oils are good for this chakra, while useful gemstones include lapis lazuli, amethyst, sodalite and sugilite. Lapis was mentioned as a cure for cataracts in writings from as early as 1600 B.C. It is said to have a natural antidepressant action, to increase awareness and raise self-esteem, while helping release creativity and self-expression. It also helps us open to psychic abilities. Amethyst helps raise spiritual awareness and open to previously unattained levels during meditation. Clarifying our vision and wisdom, and protecting us from negativity, it helps us maintain a sense of justice, fairness and peace. Sodalite also increases spiritual awareness, keeping us detached and objective and pressing us to find truth and follow our ideals. Sugilite (luvulite) helps us maintain our point of view despite pressure to change and also to help find agreement in conflict.

Now You

Now let us look at what happened at the times of development of your brow chakra, so you can bring to light that what to be healed.

Breathe. Take a few deep breaths and record what comes to mind when you focus on these times in your life. Do not worry about the later times if you haven't gotten there yet. If you are doing this work in your third focus, I honor and congratulate you!

What I remember of the time between 21 and 26 is:

_____

_____

_____

_____

_____

_____

_____

_____

We contain an inner world which is just as active and complicated as the one in which we live.
JONATHAN MILLER, M.D.

Important people of that time include (these may be family members, teachers, friends, people who loved you or people who may have hurt you):

_____   _____

_____   _____

_____   _____

_____   _____

My feelings about this time and the people are:

_____

_____

_____

_____

_____

_____

_____

_____

_____

Second Focus

What was happening in my life between ages 51 and 56:

_____

_____

_____

_____

_____

_____

_____

_____

_____

The major people in my life were:

_____   _____

_____   _____

_____   _____

_____   _____

My feelings about this time and the people are:

_____

_____

_____

_____

_____

_____

_____

_____

_____

Third Focus

What is happening in my life between ages 81 and 86:

_____

_____

_____

_____

_____

_____

_____

_____

We don't receive wisdom; we must discover it for ourselves after a journey that no one can take for us nor spare us.
MARCEL PROUST

The major people in my life are:

_____   _____

_____   _____

_____   _____

_____   _____

My feelings about this time and the people are:

_____

_____

_____

_____

_____

_____

_____

_____

> *The eye of imagination follows the rhythm of the circle. If your vision is confined to linear purpose, you may miss out on the secret destiny that a form of activity can bring you.*
> JOHN O'DONOHUE

What All This Gave Me

List here the *positive* effects on your life—for example: I had to question what I heard and saw; I had to develop my intuition; I got into starting to heal myself; I got so sick I had to get help. If you cannot see the positive effects now, just skip this section and return to it when it all makes more sense. When you do that, please do both of the meditations again, as your capacity to forgive, heal and come to inner peace will have increased significantly.

_____

_____

_____

_____

_____

_____

Now let us look at the healing or development of your brow chakra.

Exercises

These exercises will help you emotionally and physically overcome any difficulties associated with your brow chakra, and will aid its development.

Exercise One

You will need:
- ∾ One of the crystals appropriate for this chakra—preferably a small piece, appropriately cleansed
- ∾ 45 minutes of uninterrupted time
- ∾ One or two pillows and perhaps a blanket
- ∾ Your phone off the hook (and cell phone off)

This exercise will help you open your brow chakra and utilize your intuition more fully.

Go to your safe place and get comfortable lying on your back. Place a pillow under your knees if you wish to protect your back and be comfortable; cover yourself with a blanket if you wish. Hold your crystal in your left hand and close your eyes. Bring in some white light through the top of your head and breathe it down into every part of you, cleansing, healing and balancing, bringing you into harmony. Take another deep breath and, this time, bring the light down to your left hand and into the crystal you are holding. Let the light enter it and cleanse it. Now, take the crystal and place it on the middle of your forehead, slightly above and between your eyebrows. Breathe and get relaxed and comfortable.

Now take your focus to your brow chakra and allow yourself to open to your inner vision. Allow any picture to develop. Follow it and learn whatever you can. What is it telling you? Thank yourself and your crystal for helping you, then let the picture fade. Breathe. Allow another vision to develop with the intention that it will be positive and particularly significant to you. Again, follow it, appreciate it and learn whatever you can from it. Continue for as long as you can, each time giving thanks.

When you feel it is time to leave the exercise, give thanks again. Remove your crystal from your brow chakra, hold it in your hand and when you are ready put it down. Remain where you are for a while, absorbing all you can from this exercise. Then take a deep breath and either turn on your side and take a nap or gently sit up, staying grounded and drinking a little water. Stretch, note your impressions and eventually return to your day.

_____

_____

_____

_____

_____

Exercise Two

You will need:
- ❧ This book and your pen
- ❧ Some extra paper
- ❧ Your safe place
- ❧ 45 minutes of uninterrupted time

This exercise will help you change and enhance your life.

Close your eyes and imagine a clear, crystal screen, like one at the movies and on which you can create movement, close-ups and distant, panoramic shots. Choose an area of your life you would like to change and enhance—for example, a relationship, your career or your home. Now, place this chosen area on the screen and observe it in all its detail. Spend a few minutes examining it closely. Remember it.

What do you dislike about it to make you want to change it?

_____

_____

_____

_____

_____

_____

What is missing that you would like it to have?

_____

_____

_____

_____

_____

_____

_____

> *Your vision will become clear only when you can look into your own heart. Who looks outside, dreams; who looks inside, awakes.*
>
> CARL JUNG

What aspects of it would you like to keep?

_____

_____

_____

_____

_____

_____

What are your feelings about it? Allow yourself any emotion that comes up and record it along with your other findings. You may find that there are aspects of the current situation you really want to keep, and that is fine.

_____

_____

_____

_____

_____

_____

No matter how much you want to change this aspect of your life now, it has so far been beneficial to you. There are things you have gained from it—for example, coping skills, compassion, understanding—that were obviously essential to your development. With an open mind, let yourself be aware of the gifts you have received and list them here:

_____

_____

_____

_____

_____

_____

Each of us has something to do that can be done by no one else. If someone else could fulfill your destiny, then they would be in your place and you would not be here.

JOHN O'DONOHUE

Now, send gratitude to the highest place for all these things that were part of your training. If you have learned sufficiently from them, it is time to let them go.

So, take a deep breath, and as you do so, close your eyes again and visualize the same screen, but this time let the picture change.

Change any aspect you wish (you may find yourself wanting to completely wipe out the whole first picture, changing everything) and create in detail what you want. You can keep adjusting the picture until it feels right. When you feel it is perfect for the moment (you can change it again at any time), look at it closely and take the vision deeply within your heart. Then take another deep breath and open your eyes.

Record a description of what you are creating:

_____

_____

_____

_____

_____

_____

_____

_____

_____

_____

_____

_____

_____

_____

_____

_____

_____

Now take your extra paper and write a description of this aspect of your life as you intend to create it. You are now going to place this paper in the appropriate area of your room or home, according to feng shui principles (see below). You could enhance this process even further by writing on paper appropriate to the color of the area of the *bagua* or by using a colored pen.

The following diagram is a very simplified *bagua*, which will help you to work out the appropriate area to place your writing. In working out the appropriate area, imagine the lower edge of the diagram as the wall of your house or room where the main entrance is located. As you will see, each area pertains to a particular aspect of your life. For example, if the subject of this exercise has been a relationship, place your paper in the right corner furthest away from the main entrance, and so on. If you want to know more about feng shui, *Feng Shui for Beginners* by Richard Webster (Llewellyn Worldwide) would be a good place to start.

PROSPERITY (purple and gold)	**FAME** (red)	**RELATIONSHIPS** (pink or red)
FAMILY (green)	**HEALTH** (yellow or earth colors)	**CHILDREN** (yellow and white)
WISDOM AND LEARNING (blue)	**CAREER** (black)	**HELPFUL PEOPLE AND ANGELS** (silver and gray)

When you have placed the paper safely, send gratitude and use the following affirmations, which will confirm your intention:

I am welcoming this into my life now for my higher good and the higher good of all.
I offer deep, heartfelt gratitude for the positive changes that are occurring in my life
  now for my higher good and the higher good of all.

Repeat this exercise for any area of your life. Leave all of the papers in the relevant places until you feel ready to go and read them again. When you do, feel free to change things even further—maybe the handsome, brown-eyed face has become less important than sense of humor, trustworthiness and loyalty. Maybe the perfect career has moved from one that earns large amounts of money to one that gives you quality time with your family (you can ask for both of those things, however—and do not feel guilty or that you are being greedy). Whenever you make changes, send gratitude to the unseen forces of the universe that are working with you and always end with the above affirmations.

Exercise Three

You will need:
- ⤿ This book and a pen
- ⤿ A clear quartz crystal, if you have one (unless you have or have had cancer, in which case you may use amethyst instead)
- ⤿ 30 minutes of uninterrupted time

This exercise will help you develop your clairvoyant skill, although should you wish to develop this properly I recommend you have an assessment for a psychic development class and begin training.

Perhaps there is an object you cannot find—that is where we will begin. Have your crystal beside you—it may help you focus and clear your mind.

Close your eyes and allow your consciousness to be as clear as possible. Bring into your consciousness the same crystal screen you used in the last exercise. Now bring to mind the lost object and place it on the screen. Observe it in as much detail as you possibly can. Now, continue watching the screen and let a scene start to develop. At first, it might not be very detailed: you may perceive color or shape but little else. Continue to focus and allow some time for the scene to continue developing without your conscious input. Be an astute observer. You might find that you suddenly recognize some of the scene—for example, another object, part of your home or perhaps a landscape. Continue to observe carefully. When you feel there is no more information for you to gain, gently open your eyes and record below in as much detail as possible the object, the scene and any clues, which include emotions that arise.

_____

_____

_____

_____

_____

_____

_____

_____

_____

_____

Sometimes in writing the description, a flow of further information will begin and if so, record this also. If at any time you need to go back to the image to refer to it, simply close your eyes and call up the screen again. Even if you feel you have little information, try to check out what you have found. You might be surprised at what happens. Do not lose heart if little transpires the first time; this is a skill that will develop over time, though like all skills it needs practice.

As always, give thanks before you return to your daily tasks.

Exercise Four

You will need:
- ∾ A local telephone directory
- ∾ Your phone
- ∾ Your schedule or appointment book

You have worked very hard, and now it is time to reward yourself and experience the power of color in your life. You are going to spoil yourself by having a color consultation from a professional. So look in your phone book now, and at an appropriate time call and make an appointment. Using the colors that suit your complexion and personality can completely change your mood, your outlook, attitude and self-confidence. Enjoy!

Meditations

Meditation One

You will need:
- ∾ This book and your pen
- ∾ 30 minutes of uninterrupted time

Here we are at the point of vision, wisdom and command.

You have come a long way on your journey and are much clearer and healthier than you were when you began. However, there is always more work to do until it is time for us to go home. So …

Make yourself comfortable in your safe place with as much support as you need to let you physically hold your position for a while.

As always, focus first on your breathing and relax your body, letting go of anything negative through your root chakra and the soles of your feet. Let light enter in through your crown chakra and feelings of love fill and envelop you, cleansing, healing and balancing you. You feel safe and comfortable and the healing of this place is now almost automatic. Enjoy.

Now, gently loving yourself, take a deep breath and take yourself back to the age of 21 and scan the years between then and 26. Take your young adult self and wrap him/her in light and hold him/her securely.

You have already unearthed the events of this time, so now, wrap them all together ready to be healed. Take your time. When you are ready, send a wave of love and forgiveness to yourself and others, and to the events of that time.

Now, as you have done so many times before, raise yourself spiritually so you can see that whoever may have hurt you then was living out his or her own pain and process, and if you can, but only if you can, send forgiveness with love, compassion and understanding.

Then if you can, but only if you can, move to yet a higher spiritual level where you can see that whatever happened to you then was essential for your spiritual growth in this lifetime, and that those who were involved with you then were your teachers, and may have given up much in terms of the possibilities of having a good relationship with you in order to teach you what you needed to know. If you are able to acknowledge this, then perhaps you can now see that forgiveness is redundant and that gratitude is more fitting for these people who changed the course of your life. So, if you can, send them love and gratitude now and in doing so complete the lesson that your relationship with them taught you. Love, gratitude and forgiveness are the final lesson.

Take your time with this, and only go as far as you feel ready to do. Then breathe light into every part of you and allow yourself an inner smile at a job well done.

Stay here as long as you wish. When you are ready, take another deep breath and this time fill your whole being with light, love and oxygen and start to prepare for your return to the room. Become more aware of your physical presence. Move your fingers and your toes, and start to come back to a place behind your closed eyes. Make sure you are well-grounded, and when you feel fully present, gently open your eyes.

Have a stretch and a drink of water, then record whatever you wish here.

_____

_____

_____

_____

_____

_____

_____

_____

_____

_____

Take as much time as you wish before going on to the next meditation.

Meditation Two

You will need:

∾ This book and your pen

∾ 45 minutes of uninterrupted time.

Settle down into your safe place and induce that relaxed state in the usual way. Let go of anything negative through the soles of your feet and your root chakra.

Now … bring your focus to your brow chakra, slightly above and between your eyebrows. With a single loving thought bring in some beautiful light through the top of your head and allow that whole area to be cleansed. Visualize your brow chakra glowing with a wonderful deep indigo light, and as you watch, it opens further and the light increases and radiates forth from you.

Now, through the center of your brow chakra shine another light—this time white, clear and strong. This light has the ability to shine beyond the horizons of time and space.

All that is manifest in your life now—both the people and the material things, began in a different place. There were times when you could not see those who are close to you now. For a time they were beyond the horizons of time and space and you could not perceive them, despite the fact that they were making their way towards you, as you were towards them. Now there are others who are also becoming ready to enter your life.

In this moment, clear your vision and look down that wonderful beam of light shining through your brow chakra. This light is shining to a place and time that you have not yet been able to see, where there are those who are bringing you love and joy, hope and beauty, work and opportunity. They are the people of your future as you are one of the people of their future also.

Now, allow them to move towards you. Take your time and let them to take theirs. Let them come into view. You may not be able to see their faces, but you can see their form as they come bringing wonderful gifts into your life. You are taking them gifts also.

Send out a beam of love to embrace them. Send out joy and hope. Send out welcome. Send them love and the commitment that the relationship between you will be based on mutual love and respect, and that you will each play your part with compassion and understanding. Feel their welcome extended toward you also.

These may be souls you have known forever; they may be souls you have never met. But since every transaction contains a gift, the very fact that they are approaching confirms that they will prompt your growth, extend your experience and touch your heart. Everything that passed between you will be significant to your spiritual growth and theirs.

Stay a while and feel the wonderful energy between you. Perceive the love flowing between your hearts. Hold them in love. Enjoy. Stay as long as you like but eventually you need to return here and allow them the time and space to do whatever they need to do before they eventually arrive here in your life. So now send a final beam of love and light, with the promise that when you meet them it will be in love, joy and openness and with equality and a sense of brotherhood and sisterhood.

For the moment, allow them to go—to recede once more to where they need to be in their lives right now. They will come at the perfect time.

For now, give thanks and gently allow the beam of love and light to be reabsorbed into your brow chakra. Breathe deeply and be aware of this time and place and that this is where you belong right now. Take another deep breath and fill your cells with oxygen, and in doing so become more aware of your physical presence. Allow your brow chakra to close to where it is most comfortable. You can open it again whenever you wish.

Take another deep breath and make sure you are grounded. Gently move your fingers and your toes, and when you are ready, open your eyes.

Have a drink of water and stretch, then record whatever you wish below.

_____

_____

_____

_____

_____

_____

_____

_____

_____

_____

Affirmations

I open to fully utilize the gift of my intuition.

I see the world with spiritual eyes and welcome all the gifts that are prepared for me.

I take command of my life and move forward now to manifest an abundant future.

Make your own affirmations

_____

_____

_____

_____

_____

_____

Notes

CHAPTER SEVEN

The Crown Chakra

Behold,
the mellow light that floods the eastern sky.
In signs of praise both heaven and earth unite.
And from the fourfold manifested powers a chant of love arises,
both from the flaming fire and the flowing water,
and from sweet-smelling earth and from rustling wind,
from the deep unfathomable vortex of that golden light
in which the victor bathes,
all nature's wordless voice in a thousand tones arises to proclaim:
Joy unto you, O men of Earth.
A pilgrim has returned back from the other shore.
A conscious being is born.

VEDIC TRADITION

The upper end of the central power channel is the crown chakra, the so-called thousand-lotus blossom chakra. Here we open fully to our spirituality, to unity consciousness and to our divinity. This chapter is different from the rest since there are no dysfunctions at the crown chakra. We either develop it and open ourselves to its glories, or we are not ready for its wonder and remain closed and unable to fully connect with the Divine. Whether or not it is developed, we can still visualize light coming in through it and utilize the healing light from the Divine.

For some people, working on the crown chakra is a life's work. Though we may talk of spirituality or be religious, it is only in developing and opening the crown that we can feel almost constantly—or certainly within moments of the intention—the flood of ecstatic energy that heralds our connection. This is that natural high we call spiritual ecstasy that we may have known for a split second before. Even though it may take you a while to perfect (it needs *all* our chakras to be in good shape), now, with the development of the crown, be prepared for an experience that will change you forever and fill you with simultaneous joy and reverence and flood you with love for everything and everyone.

So let us look at the crown chakra and how you are going to achieve this wonderful gift.

What You Can Hope to Gain by Working with Your Crown Chakra

- A conscious connection with the Divine
- A sense of alignment and perfect clarity
- The gift of healing
- Inner peace
- A new sense of wonder at all the Universe
- Freedom to be all that you are

Now, take a look at the following questions and assess for yourself the work you would like to do here.

SELF-ASSESSMENT QUESTIONNAIRE

❑ 1. Do you have a sense of being called to do healing or be involved in some mystical art?

❑ 2. Do you wish to be more enlightened and have a sense of oneness with all things?

❑ 3. Do you want to be able to feel a sense of euphoric bliss not induced by anything external?

❑ 4. Can you, or do you want to see everyone as equal and part of universal consciousness?

❑ 5. Do you want to have a direct everpresent connection with the Divine?

❑ 6. Do you want to see all of life with endless love and compassion?

❑ 7. Do you want to be able to see everything in absolute simplicity and wonder?

❑ 8. Do you want to be aware of divine order in all things, including your desire to change it?

❑ 9. Would you like to be able to forgive with love, understanding, compassion and even gratitude while nevertheless striving for justice?

❑ 10. Would you like to radiate love and peace to all things?

❑ 11. Would you like to feel perfectly aligned, supported by the earth and connected with the Divine?

❑ 12. Would you like to be able to live simultaneously your humanity and your divinity?

❑ 13. Would you like to live all your gifts and enjoy life to the full?

If you answer "yes" to most of the above, then you will enjoy developing your crown chakra. The development of the crown chakra and realization of its wonders is a delightful ongoing, lifelong task. Let us learn more about it so you can start to heal it if necessary and embark on its development.

❧ BASICS OF THE CROWN CHAKRA ❧

SITE: The crown chakra is situated above the head and extends up to open at the edge of the causal body.

COLOR: In some people the developed crown chakra is white and in others it is deep purple.

ACTIVATION AND DEVELOPMENT: It may be activated at any time, though classically our focus comes to the crown between 26 and 30 and again between 56 and 60 and 86 and 90. However, in some people it opens spontaneously even in childhood, though in many people it hardly develops at all until perhaps the last few moments before death, when we realize the full extent of our consciousness and divinity. Usually we need to make a conscious effort to open and develop our crown chakra; otherwise it may remain like a closed door to a wonderful palace that we have never thought to explore.

SPECIAL CONNECTIONS: Though the crown chakra integrates the whole system, to some extent it has a special connection with the root chakra, since it is at the higher end of the central power channel, whereas the root is at the lower end. They both open onto the causal body, unlike the other chakras, which open at the level of the emotional body.

ASSOCIATED SENSE: There is no associated sense as such.

GLANDULAR ASSOCIATION: It is associated with the pituitary, pineal and the hypothalamus. The hypothalamus secretes hormones that regulate the hormonal flow from the pituitary, which in turn orchestrates the whole endocrine system. The hormones of the anterior lobe of the pituitary stimulate the other glands in the endocrine system, while those of the posterior lobe stimulate the uterus to contract during pregnancy and also the breast to produce milk. The pineal gland secretes melatonin.

NEUROLOGICAL CONNECTION: The crown chakra is associated with the cerebral cortex, which commands the whole neurological system.

ASSOCIATED AURIC BODY: The causal body, which is golden and egg-shaped, extends 72 to 80 inches from the physical body. It holds within it past life bands, which eventually disappear as we resolve karmic issues.

❧ FUNCTIONS OF THE CROWN CHAKRA ❧

UNITY, UNIVERSAL, CHRIST, OR BUDDHA CONSCIOUSNESS: The crown chakra lifts us to the awareness of the simultaneous absolute simplicity and complexity of universal consciousness where we are each unique and individual souls yet we are all one; where we are simultaneously human and divine; where we can control nothing, yet everything is in perfect divine order; where there is a limitless, boundless nothingness that encompasses everything; where there is no space between us and yet there is only space; where we are physical human beings of substance and yet spiritual beings made only of light; where consciousness is invisible and yet visible in everything there is.

UNDERSTANDING: This understanding of unity consciousness takes us beyond anything we could learn with our intelligence, surmise with logic or compute with our human brain.

PEACE, ECSTASY AND BLISS: At the crown chakra we can transcend all we have known thus far. We can program ourselves to reach the unreachable, to touch the untouchable and to find, albeit initially only for tiny snatches of time, absolute peace, where everything is suspended and we know the bliss of utter awareness—we are in spiritual ecstasy.

TRANSFORMATION: Learning to enter this blissful state of spiritual ecstasy, hold it and incorporate it into our human life, something wondrous happens to us. We are transformed—permanently changed—and this change is perceptible not only to us, but to those around us. We have glimpsed and experienced heaven and we can never be the same again.

RADIATING LOVE AND PEACE: Mastering the art of working with the energy of the crown brings us calm and serenity and the capacity to radiate universal love to all those around us, while remaining ordinary human beings, doing ordinary things with our feet on the ground. We are not expected to float around constantly in a state of beatific peace. We are human beings and it is part of our business on earth to feel our emotions and learn to deal with them while still remaining unconditionally loving to all.

KNOWLEDGE AND TRUTH: We talked of truth at the throat chakra, and here at the crown we become even more aware of the fact that, just as a seed contains the whole template of the plant, and the strand of DNA holds the key to the whole person, this moment holds all the truth and all the knowledge there ever was and ever shall be. All we have to do is find it. We are all at different points on the path; we all have our own understanding of the truth, but here at the crown we move towards our primary goal of reaching the point of knowing.

ENLIGHTENMENT: Here at the crown, we can finally be free of the constraints of our human brain, and can immerse ourselves in truth and knowing as we transcend and are at one again with the great body of consciousness, the divine source we may call God. Here at last we can understand as we surrender with simultaneous power and humility to that which is so much greater than us and yet of which we are a powerful part.

ALIGNMENT: Alignment occurs when all of our chakras are developed, clear and unobstructed, forming a clear channel that allows a breeze of energy to blow up and down through them all, bringing us simultaneously robust energy from the earth and spiritual energy from the cosmos. This energy nurtures us on all levels, constantly; though especially when we meditate. And in this connection with the Divine, we become who we really are—humanity and divinity in perfect manifestation and balance.

Oils and Gemstones for the Crown Chakra

Amber is the choice of oil or incense for the crown chakra, and though diamonds would be the classic gemstone, clear quartz, amethyst, labradorite (spectorolite) and celestite are all wonderful. As always, if you have or have had cancer, please do not use clear quartz. It can enhance any of the functions of the crown chakra listed above and stimulates the swift ascent from the brow to the crown, quickening the manifestation of psychic and spiritual gifts. As I said in the last chapter, amethyst helps raise spiritual awareness and open to previously unattained levels during meditation. Clarifying our vision and wisdom, and protecting from negativity, it helps us maintain a sense of justice and fairness and peace. Labradorite (spectorolite) has the same frequency as the crown chakra and helps it clear, open and develop, stimulating channeling and intuition. It also helps us clear debris obstructing our ascent and helps us with telepathy and inspiration. Celestite cleanses and balances the aura, suffusing our energy body with light and love during meditation and enabling us to make and hold our conscious connection with the divine.

Now You

Let us have a look at the times of natural development of your crown chakra so you can bring to mind anything that needs to be cleared, forgiven or healed. In doing this, you will have looked at all of your life in terms of your chakra development, and though you may need to go back again to clear other things that come up, you will have tilled the ground and made much easier the task of healing the whole you.

So …

Take a few deep breaths and record what comes to mind when you focus on these times in your life. Once again, I have added the third focus, just in case. However, if you are doing this work at that focus, please write to me! (Of course, anyone is welcome to write to me.)

What I remember of the time between 26 and 30 is:

We choose our next world through what we learn in this one. Learn nothing, and the next world is the same as this one, all the same limitations and lead weights to overcome.

RICHARD BACH

Important people of that time include (these may be family members, teachers, friends, people who loved you or people who may have hurt you):

My feelings about this time and the people are:

_____

_____

_____

_____

_____

_____

_____

_____

_____

Second Focus

What was happening in my life between ages 56 and 60:

_____

_____

_____

_____

_____

_____

_____

_____

You are precious and honored in my sight and I love you.
PSALM 43

The major people in my life were:

My feelings about this time and the people are:

_____

_____

_____

_____

_____

_____

_____

_____

_____

When you close your doors, and make darkness within, remember never to say that you are alone, for you are not alone; nay, God is within and your genius is within. And what need have they of light to see what you are doing.

EPICTETUS

Third Focus

What is happening in my life between ages 86 and 90:

_____

_____

_____

_____

_____

_____

_____

_____

_____

_____

The major people in my life are:

My feelings about this time and the people are:

_____

_____

_____

_____

_____

_____

_____

_____

Now let us start to clear and develop your crown chakra.

Exercises

Exercise One

This exercise is in three parts.
You will need:
- ∽ Your pen and this book
- ∽ Some colored pens
- ∽ Perhaps some extra paper
- ∽ At least one hour of uninterrupted time for Part 1 and 45 minutes for Part 2

When I do Part 3 of this—which I do regularly because I just love the feeling and clarity of it—I choose the afternoon or early evening because I then want to have the rest of the day alone with the Divine, so feel free to do the first part and then schedule a different time for the visualization.

> *You created my innermost self,*
> *Knit me together in my mother's womb.*
> *For so many marvels I thank you;*
> *A wonder am I, and all your works are wonders.*
> PSALM 139

PART 1

Thus far we have been looking at the chakra system bit by bit to understand its functions, its gifts and why it might not have been working as well as it could. But now let us bring everything together and look at the whole system and what you have achieved so far.

> *The root of the word Buddha means to wake up, to know, to understand; and he who wakes up and understands is called a Buddha. It is as simple as that. The capacity to wake up, to understand, to love is called Buddha nature …*
> THICH NHAT HANH

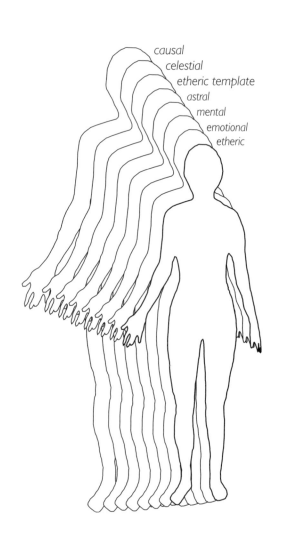

causal
celestial
etheric template
astral
mental
emotional
etheric

Using your colored pens, mark on the diagram what you have achieved so far—I have put in just a few key words for each chakra. Then refer back to the chapter earlier or to the relevant chapter in *The 7 Healing Chakras* to see what you can hope to gain, and mark, in a different color, qualities you are still working on. If you wish, you could make a copy of this diagram and put it on the front of your fridge or in your desk drawer and add to it, as you perceive changes in the way you behave and the ways you perceive the world.

PART 2

Though we have talked little of the auric bodies apart from naming and describing them, let us now add them.

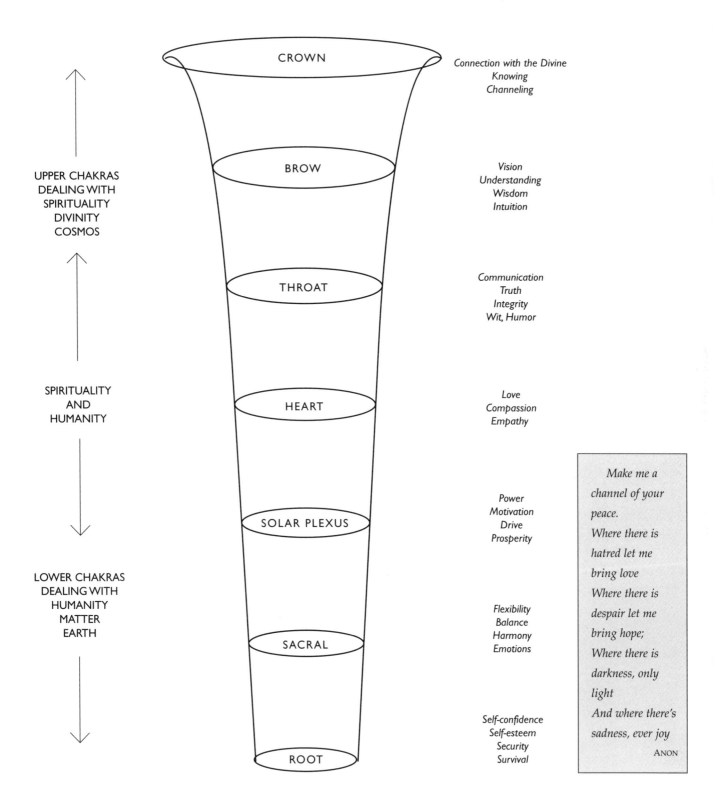

UPPER CHAKRAS
DEALING WITH
SPIRITUALITY
DIVINITY
COSMOS

SPIRITUALITY
AND
HUMANITY

LOWER CHAKRAS
DEALING WITH
HUMANITY
MATTER
EARTH

CROWN — *Connection with the Divine / Knowing / Channeling*

BROW — *Vision / Understanding / Wisdom / Intuition*

THROAT — *Communication / Truth / Integrity / Wit, Humor*

HEART — *Love / Compassion / Empathy*

SOLAR PLEXUS — *Power / Motivation / Drive / Prosperity*

SACRAL — *Flexibility / Balance / Harmony / Emotions*

ROOT — *Self-confidence / Self-esteem / Security / Survival*

> *Make me a channel of your peace.*
> *Where there is hatred let me bring love*
> *Where there is despair let me bring hope;*
> *Where there is darkness, only light*
> *And where there's sadness, ever joy*
> ANON

An insult at any level causes disruption of the system—for example, an injury to the body can cause emotional, psychological and spiritual upset, and similarly an insult to the soul can eventually cause dis-ease on the physical level. In healing, therefore, we need to address the whole—body, mind and soul.

Look at the whole system now. Perhaps you can see how things that happened years ago have affected you, made you sick, kept you stuck and prevented you from standing up and being all you can be. However, as always, bear in mind that these things were part of your training, and that the wisdom and clarity they brought could not have been achieved in any other way. So if you need to, let them go once again, and forgive. If in looking at this diagram you are able to see more of your bigger picture, it might be a good time to go back and add to the section in each chapter about what you have gained from what happened in your life. For example, you may not be sitting here doing this work and being on the verge of a huge awakening had you not suffered earlier; or you may see that this life experience has acquitted you well for training as a healer.

Take your time, and if there feels to be too much to do at one sitting, come back to it when you are ready. However, make sure you are well-grounded when you leave each time.

PART 3

A couple of notes . . .

1. You may find it difficult at first to see all the colors and perceive the whole of your being. Do not worry! For the moment, just go through the process—you may be surprised at what happens. But if you're like me, you will come back to this again and again as part of your spiritual practice and eventually you will see yourself fully expanded and in glorious Technicolor!

2. Although I have suggested you move from one auric body out to the next to achieve a full sense of your magnificence, in fact all of them may be fused and superimposed rather than lying loosely around each other or extending out from each other. This I find difficult to put into words. However, the visualization works very well and the rest will come in time.

3. Please take your time throughout and stop, explore and wonder wherever you wish. Then also take time with giving gratitude. I often stay here for ages, being unwilling to drag myself away because I feel so awestruck and filled with gratitude that I just don't want to leave.

4. Your need for oxygen will reduce and your breathing may become quite shallow. This is nothing to worry about, but you may find yourself taking a huge gulp of air at the end. I have put a prompt here and there to remind you to breathe!

> *Plan by all means, but let the Divine have the details.*
> Brenda Davies

Now, with your eyes closed, visualize your whole physical body. Feel it, perceive it, sense it, explore it and breathe into it. Let your breath be focused on each of your organs and let them have an inner smile in gratitude for supporting your humanity.

Now take your focus inside and visualize your central power channel running down the length of your spine and, taking your time at every stage, starting at the bottom of the channel, visualize each of your chakras leading from it:

❧ your root chakra spinning down into the earth, deep and rich red

❧ then your sacral—in front of you and behind you, translucent orange

∾ now your solar plexus, in front of you and behind you, bright yellow

∾ then come up to your heart, in front of you and behind you, green or pink

∾ then to your throat, blue light, horizontal at the front but raising slightly at an angle at the back of your neck

∾ then your brow, deep indigo or purple light in front of you and behind you

∾ now visualize your wonderful crown chakra, white or purple above your head, extending from the top of the central power channel

Feel the energy of each chakra. Feel the wonderful energy in the central power channel—the deep robust energy of the earth coming in at the root chakra and mingling with the fine light-energy coming in at the crown. Just stay with that for a moment and try moving the energy up and down and perceiving what happens.

And now … taking your time at every stage …

Be aware again of your physical body and then extend your focus to about an inch outside your skin. This is your etheric body and is associated closely with your physical body. It is bluish-gray, pulsating constantly and flowing around the contours of your body and also every organ, bathing them and nurturing them.

Now extend your focus out a little further, out into your emotional body. Its energy is lighter and it appears as clouds of pastel colors, constantly flowing into each other and around you, extending to about three to four inches from your body. It governs your emotions. Breathe love and light into it now and fill yourself with peace. Feel your inner harmony and balance.

Take a breath and move your focus out into your mental body—yellow and strong, shining all around you four to eight inches from your body, holding you in your own power. Take your time.

Now extend your focus out into your astral body—clouds of beautiful color, extending to about 18–24 inches from your body. It is probably pink around your heart as you now breathe love to your whole being. If you think of someone you particularly love you may see it go pink in other places too.

Take your time, then move your focus again. Now you enter your etheric template or ketheric body. Blue and silver, it holds the perfect template of your physical body and no matter what happens to you it will continue to hold you in perfection. Your focus may now extend to about 24–30 inches from your body.

Remember to breathe.

And now you approach your celestial body—shafts of pastel-colored light extending away from you, scintillating constantly. Feel now your wisdom, understanding and intuition. It may extend to about 40 inches from your body. Take time to enjoy, and then …

Keeping yourself well-grounded, extend your focus now into your causal body. Feel yourself fully expanded, and perceive your whole causal body, golden and magnificent, extending up to 60 or more inches from your physical body.

Enjoy this feeling of expanding into your whole being and witnessing simultaneously your physical body and the light of your soul. This is you! You are not only a strong, healthy human but also a magnificent spiritual being.

Do not forget to breathe!

The body desires green herbs and running water, because its origin is from those. The soul desires life and the Living One, because its origin is the Infinite Soul. The desire of the soul is for knowledge and wisdom; the desire of the body is for orchard, meadows and vines. The desire of the soul is for ascent and sublimity; the desire of the body is for gain and the means of self-indulgence.

RUMI

Give yourself time to explore this wonderful world that is you. Allow any emotion that comes up to be experienced and let it pass.

Breathe deeply and give thanks—thanks to the earth for holding you and supporting you; thanks to the Divine for being ever-open to you, and ask that you will always be well-protected. Visualize a golden coat around your causal body protecting every bit of you.

This is your reality—it is not going to disappear, so when you are ready, taking your time, gently bring your focus back from your causal body, leaving it well-protected, to your celestial body, then through your ketheric body to the astral and from there to the mental. Come back through your emotional body and finally your etheric, and focus now on your physical body. Breathe light into every part of it and let anything that needs to heal do so. Give thanks.

Stay as long as you wish. When you are ready, take a nice deep breath and fill your physical body with oxygen. Start to be aware of your physical presence—move your fingers and toes and then start to come back to a place behind your closed eyes. When you feel fully aware, gently open your eyes and be fully present. Make sure you are well-grounded.

Record whatever you wish here and continue on a spare sheet of paper if you need to.

_____

_____

_____

_____

_____

_____

_____

_____

_____

_____

_____

_____

_____

_____

_____

_____

_____

Let us see to it that our lives, like jewels of great price, be noteworthy not because of their width, but because of their weight. Let us measure them by their per-formance, not their duration.
SENECA

_____

_____

_____

_____

Like the bee gathering honey from different flowers, the wise man accepts the essence of different scriptures and sees only the good in all religions.

SRIMAD
BHAGAVATAM

Exercise Two

This is your chance to try channeling …

You will need:

❧ An hour of uninterrupted time—best not to schedule anything soon after this

❧ This book and your pen

❧ A separate book that you may wish to call your channeling diary or something similar

❧ A recording device or a friend you can trust to just be there and scribe for you (but without making any comment and certainly without bursting into laughter!)

A HANDY TIP!

While you are channeling do not worry about what you are saying, what is happening, how accurate it might be or that you might be making a fool of yourself! Just report it as it is. Sometimes I have reported things that appear to make no sense but turn out to be significant to someone else. Try not to interfere with the process or you will lose the connection. Please respect the sanctity of the process, and until you have mastered the art, do not attempt to channel anything for anyone else. No party games please!

Prepare yourself and get comfortable, sitting with your back as erect as you can manage.

Now, visualize your central power channel open and clear. At its base, get yourself well-grounded. Be aware of the wonder of what you are about to do.

Ask that you will receive only the highest wisdom from the highest possible source and commit to treating it with reverence and to use it only for your higher good or for the higher good of all. Switch on your recording device or have your friend be ready with pen and paper.

Now, allow yourself to stand aside while, with a single thought, you open your crown chakra. Be willing to wait and be open without trying to make anything happen. Be ready to simply open your throat and speak or open your eyes and write. Sometimes, as the flow begins, you may try to grasp it, or start to question it, and you will find yourself suddenly bumping back to the ordinary world, often feeling a bit foolish because you do not really know what you were talking about. If this happens, just gently get grounded, re-establish the connection and start again. Even when the channeling begins, you may find that you have a stream of consciousness flow through you, then it seems to stop and you lose the connection. Do not worry. Just center yourself again, and on you go.

When you feel it is over for now, or you are tired and want to stop, all you have to do is to have that thought and move back into place, as it were, and there you are. Give thanks. Gently allow your crown chakra to close and make sure you are grounded again. Take as long as you need to open your eyes—you may wish to do so with your eyes downcast, since it is sometimes a bit of a shock to see bright colors or the ordinariness of your surroundings. Blink a little if this is the case for you and take a deep breath. Have a drink of water, and when you feel ready, stretch a little and walk around your room. Take your time before you do anything else.

Record here whatever you wish.

_____

_____

_____

_____

_____

_____

_____

_____

_____

_____

God does not die on the day that we cease to believe in a personal deity, but we die on the day when our lives cease to be illumined by the steady radiance, renewed daily, of a wonder, the source of which is beyond all reason.

DAG
HAMMARSKJOLD

Final Meditation

Go to your safe place and take with you anything you wish. Though you may want to prepare yourself with some music, the best thing for the crown chakra is silence. Now ... as usual, focus on your breathing, take time to relax your body and let go of anything negative you do not need in this moment.

Visualize yourself in all your majesty with your central power channel clear and your lower chakras healthy and spinning. Make sure you are grounded, and with great respect and reverence take your focus up to your crown chakra, with a single loving thought letting it open, visualizing it as a beautiful crown of light above your head. Allow it to open, see it increase in circumference and feel the wonder and beauty of it. With a thought and a breath, extend it now—pure, shining, powerful yet gentle. Then, through it, send love from your heart—deeply felt, pure love and with it your gratitude—and feel a channel form between you and the divine source of all there is. And as your love extends to the highest point, feel the warmth and amazing joy of receiving also. Welcome divine light and love—tender, powerful, all embracing, all-comforting—down the channel and feel yourself expand as you lift to complete your connection with the Divine. Feel your radiance increase as the love fills you. Feel yourself expand even further and note what is happening in your chest as divine light and love mingle with your human love. Feel the wonder.

Now take your focus to your brow and here perceive both the love and the light change to deep blue or violet. Feel yourself filled with wisdom and understanding … let it flow down to your throat where it changes to a beautiful sky blue or turquoise … feel yourself filled with creativity, truth and integrity. Know your mission …

Take your time and absorb all you can, then let it flow down to your heart, where this time it changes again to pink. Feel yourself filled and overflowing with unconditional love for yourself and for all the universe. Know compassion for everything and everyone and, without sympathy, empathize with all beings. Let your heart open with this love and radiate it out to the whole world—to those you know and love, to those you will never know but with whom you are connected in universal consciousness; to those you may have felt did not deserve your love and those who may never be able to respond to it or return it. Enjoy.

Now let it flow on down to your solar plexus where it becomes brilliant yellow. Feel yourself filled with power as your will is reinforced and you accept responsibility for the great being that you are. Feel you energy rise and know that you may be motivated to do whatever you wish and that you can have a constant flow of whatever positive energy you choose, as long as you are to use it for your higher good and the higher good of all.

Let the light move on down to your sacral chakra where it becomes bright orange. Feel yourself as a powerful sensual, sexual being, fully balanced, capable of relating to the whole world.

And finally, let the divine love and light become ruby red as it fills your root chakra, holding you secure in your own being and in the tender embrace of the earth and the cosmos.

Now, see yourself in all your radiance. See who you really are and allow yourself a mixture of pride and humility at the amazing creature you have become while still being a small part of a wondrous whole.

Breathe. Breathe in the power and the majesty. Be who you are. Feel yourself fully alive. Just be …

Let the energies flow through you and around you and let yourself be totally healed.

Let no one ever take this from you. This is who you are.

Stay as long as you wish. When you are ready, move your focus up through each chakra. Leave your root chakra open but, holding the love, close down the others a little until you feel comfortable. Lastly, send gratitude again and gently let go of the beam of light holding all its healing power as you gently close your crown chakra. Do not worry—you can come back and do this again whenever you choose.

Gently place around yourself some gentle but powerful protection—you could imagine a velvet cloak wrapped around you, or a golden halo around your causal body—then once again begin to feel your physical presence. Take a deep breath and gently move your fingers and your toes. Start to come back to a place behind your closed eyes. When you feel fully present, gently open your eyes.

Behold, I stand at the door and knock; if anyone hears my voice and opens the door, I will come to him and eat with him and he with me.
REVELATIONS 3.20

Have some water and be sure you are grounded. Stretch and move around your room a little, then record whatever you wish below.

_____

_____

_____

_____

_____

> *A person is neither a thing nor a process but an opening or clearing through which the Absolute can manifest.*
> MARTIN
> HEIDEGGER

_____

_____

_____

_____

_____

_____

_____

_____

Affirmations

These are all yours—make as many as you wish.

_____

_____

_____

_____

_____

_____

Notes

> The winds of
> God's grace are
> always blowing;
> it is for us to
> raise the sails.
>
> ASCRIBED TO
> RAMAKRISHNA

Other Ulysses Press Mind/Body Titles

THE 7 HEALING CHAKRAS: UNLOCKING YOUR BODY'S ENERGY CENTERS
Dr. Brenda Davies, $14.95
A companion to this workbook, *The 7 Healing Chakras* explores the essence of chakras—vortices of energy that connect the physical body with the spiritual.

UNLOCKING THE HEART CHAKRA: HEAL YOUR RELATIONSHIPS WITH LOVE
Dr. Brenda Davies, $14.95
Applying the techniques of the chakra system, this book examines the central relationships in our lives and offers a plan for understanding them.

CHAKRA POWER BEADS:
TAPPING THE POWER OF HEALING STONES TO UNLOCK YOUR INNER POTENTIAL
Dr. Brenda Davies, $9.95
Explains how to improve health, spirit and fortune by fully harnessing the power of beads.

ANAM CARA WISDOM: SPIRITUAL GUIDANCE FROM YOUR PERSONAL CELTIC ANGEL
Donald McKinney, $14.95
This illuminating guide explains how to form a personal relationship with one's Celtic angel and make that angel a source of protection, comfort, wisdom, and guidance.

BE YOUR OWN PSYCHIC: TAPPING THE INNATE POWER WITHIN
Sherron Mayes, $13.95
Offers lessons on understanding and programming dreams, acting on hunches, gaining true insight, and following a deeper guidance.

BUDDHA IN YOUR BACKPACK: EVERYDAY BUDDHISM FOR TEENS
Franz Metcalf, $12.95
Especially written for teenagers, *Buddha in Your Backpack* explains Buddhism and shows how Buddha's teachings can add a little wisdom and sanity to their high-velocity lives.

HOW MEDITATION HEALS: SCIENTIFIC EVIDENCE AND PRACTICAL APPLICATION
2nd edition, Eric Harrison, $14.95
In straightforward, practical terms, *How Meditation Heals* reveals how and why meditation improves the natural functioning of the human body.

FLIP THE SWITCH: 40 ANYTIME, ANYWHERE MEDITATIONS IN 5 MINUTES OR LESS
Eric Harrison, $10.95
Specially designed meditations that fit any situation: idling at a red light, waiting for a computer to restart, or standing in line at the grocery store.

JESUS AND BUDDHA: THE PARALLEL SAYINGS

Marcus Borg, Editor   Introduction by Jack Kornfield, $14.00

This book traces the life stories and beliefs of Jesus and Buddha, then presents a comprehensive collection of their remarkably similar teachings on facing pages.

JOURNEY TO TIBET'S LOST LAMA

Gaby Naher, $14.95

A personal, spiritual, and historical journey to the exiled 17th Karmapa and into the fascinating culture of Tibet and its Lama heritage.

SENSES WIDE OPEN: THE ART & PRACTICE OF LIVING IN YOUR BODY

Johanna Putnoi, $14.95

Through simple, accessible exercises, this book shows how to be at ease with yourself and experience genuine pleasure in your physical connection to others and the world.

PORTABLE REIKI: EASY SELF-TREATMENTS FOR HOME, WORK AND ON THE GO

Tanmaya Honervogt, $14.95

Presents do-it-yourself, step-by-step treatments for quick, effective Reiki healing—anytime, anyplace. The book's system is specially designed to help busy people release stress, improve health and restore personal energy.

PSYCHIC SHIELD: THE PERSONAL HANDBOOK OF PSYCHIC PROTECTION

Caitlín Matthews, $14.95

Psychic Shield provides simple and commonsense strategies for overcoming negative thinking, dealing with difficult people, becoming attuned to spiritual guidance, and protecting one's inner peace.

TEACH YOURSELF TO MEDITATE IN 10 SIMPLE LESSONS: DISCOVER RELAXATION AND CLARITY OF MIND IN JUST MINUTES A DAY

Second Edition, Eric Harrison, $13.95

Ideal for beginning students, this book guides the reader through a series of core meditations that the author has carefully honed over the years while personally guiding his students.

To order these books call 800-377-2542 or 510-601-8301, fax 510-601-8307, e-mail ulysses@ ulyssespress.com, or write to Ulysses Press, P.O. Box 3440, Berkeley, CA 94703. All retail shipped free of charge. California residents must include sales tax. Allow two to ks for delivery.

About the Author

∾

DR. BRENDA DAVIES, a British psychiatrist and spiritual healer, combines her traditional medical training with ancient healing gifts. Having lived and worked around the world, she now resides in Zambia, though her workshops, clients and conferences keep her on an international circuit. A mother of two and grandmother of one, she is happily living her own spiritual path while exploring the frontiers of love and healing. She is the author of six books, including *The 7 Healing Chakras* and *Unlocking the Heart Chakra*. For more information on Brenda's books, workshops and healing products, visit www.justbe.org.